MORE THAN PETTICOATS

Remarkable COLORADO WOMEN

Second Edition

Gayle C. Shirley

TWODOT®

GUILFORD, CONNECTICUT
HELENA, MONTANA

For Corbett Sionainn, living proof that Colorado continues to produce remarkable women.

———◦●●◦———

A · TWODOT® · BOOK

Copyright © 2002, 2012 by Rowman & Littlefield

Map by Daniel Lloyd © Rowman & Littlefield

Library of Congress Cataloging-in-Publication Data is available on file.

ISBN 978-0-7627-6444-0

Printed in the United States of America

Distributed by NATIONAL BOOK NETWORK

CONTENTS

———◆◆———

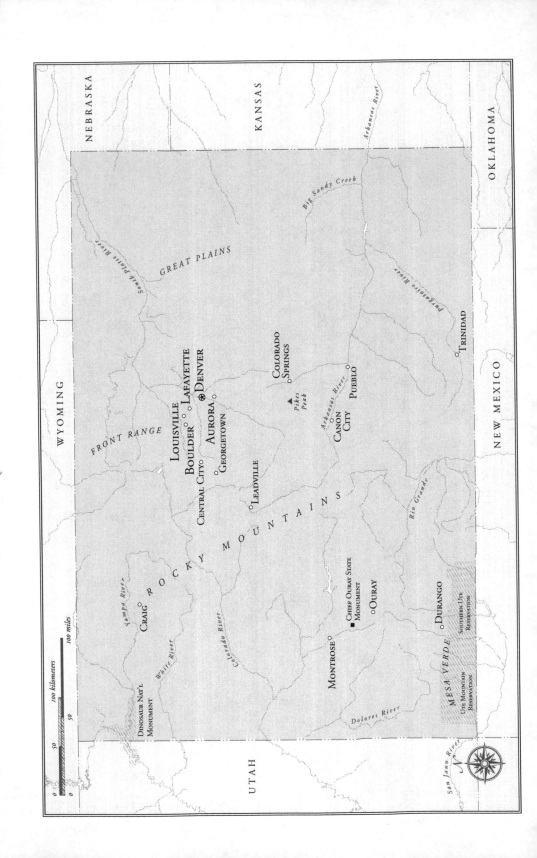

ACKNOWLEDGMENTS

I am grateful for the assistance of the following:

The staff of the Lewis and Clark County Library in Helena, Montana, was always courteous and helpful in looking for the many books and articles I requested through its interlibrary loan program.

The staffs of the Western History Department of the Denver Public Library, the Colorado Historical Society, and the Uintah County Library Regional History Center in Vernal, Utah, were very helpful in nailing down elusive details and providing photographs of these remarkable women.

Gerald R. Armstrong of the Rocky Mountain Fuel Company in Denver liberally offered information on Josephine Roche.

Millie Arvidson, manager of Matchless Mine–Baby Doe Tabor Museum at Leadville, provided information on Baby Doe and the museum.

Staff members at Dinosaur National Monument, the Molly Brown Museum in Denver, and the Ute Indian Museum in Montrose were also helpful.

INTRODUCTION

There is an adage that men *make* history, but women *are* history. That certainly was the case for all too many generations. For two centuries after our forefathers gave birth to our nation, presumably without the help of foremothers, every American student studied a history made up of kings, presidents, emperors, and generals. History books were laden with patrilineal family trees, etchings of famous male warriors and leaders, and maps of battlefields where men slaughtered other men as they conquered new lands.

But in the 1960s and 1970s, women did make history. In the course of what became known as the Feminist Revolution, they demanded recognition for their value and contributions—today, tomorrow, and yesterday. In the decades since, historians have begun taking a serious look at the role women played in building our nation. Eventually, they trained their spotlights on women of the West—those who came by steamboat, train, and covered wagon, and those who were here already.

At first, scholars shuffled western women into convenient pigeonholes. There was the idealized "Madonna of the prairies," a long-suffering pioneer wife and mother who gamely toiled across the Great Plains in calico and sunbonnet. There was the disreputable "soiled dove," an enterprising floozy who made her living in hurdy-gurdys and houses of ill repute. And there were the maiden schoolmarms, the servile "squaws," and the pistol-packing Calamity Janes.

But as historians unearthed letters and diaries left behind by flesh-and-blood frontier women, and as they learned more about the American Indian and Hispanic women who were here even earlier, they discovered that there were no convenient stereotypes. The women of the Old West were as diverse as the Colorado mountains and plains. They came from different backgrounds, had different experiences, and responded to frontier life in different ways.

For some, the move West was like taking off a corset—very liberating. The frontier offered new chances to express their individuality. For another group of women, the West was a land of privation and hardship, where the struggle to survive overwhelmed other desires. Still other women attempted to make the West an extension of the life they knew back East. They brought with them all the repressive baggage of the "cult of true womanhood," which demanded that they be pious, pure, submissive, and domestic.

"If there is one truth about frontierswomen," one historian contends, "it is that they were not any one thing."

This wealth of diversity is apparent in this book, which celebrates many remarkable women who made their mark on Colorado history.

One hazard inherent in writing about the past is the tendency to view historical events from a contemporary perspective. Yet, how can we do otherwise? We're all products of our times. Values and attitudes change, and what may have been socially acceptable a century ago may not now be "politically correct." This is especially apparent with regard to women and minorities.

I've tried to keep modern sensibilities in mind as I've written this book—but not at the expense of historical accuracy. For how can we judge how far we've come if we refuse to acknowledge where we've been? The fact is, women and minorities were considered inferior a century ago, an attitude that may be reflected in some of the quotations I use in this book. That we know better today doesn't mean that it's our job to erase incidents of sexism and racism from our history books and pretend they never happened. Our responsibility, I believe, is to recognize them for what they were and demonstrate with our own behavior that civilization has made progress.

When I began work on this book, my first challenge was to identify a dozen or so women who were worthy of inclusion in it. I wondered if I could find enough. But as I dug into historical archives, I developed a new worry: How was I to decide which of the countless fascinating Colorado women to include? How could I be sure I wouldn't overlook someone important?

To keep the book a manageable size, I chose to limit it to women born before 1900. I also tried to choose a cross section of women who excelled in various fields—from journalism and charity to business and science. Some were feminists and activists, but others simply were women without political agendas who stood out among their peers.

Obviously, I couldn't include all of Colorado's remarkable early-day women. Among the intriguing people I left out were Emily Griffith, who founded Denver's famous Opportunity School; Helen Hunt Jackson, who wrote *Ramona* and other popular books; Josephine Meeker, who survived a kidnapping by Ute Indians; Dr. Susan Anderson, who provided health care—often free—to Fraser Valley residents for almost half a century; Katherine Lee Bates, who wrote "America the Beautiful" after being inspired by the view from the top of Pikes Peak in 1893; and Mary Cronin, the first woman to climb all fifty-one Colorado peaks over fourteen thousand feet high. This book also could have featured at least two former Colorado residents who starred on the international stage: Golda Meir, Israel's fourth prime minister, and former First Lady Mamie Dowd Eisenhower. All these women—and many more—have fascinating stories, and I regret having to leave any of them out.

The fact is that most of the women who helped to shape Colorado were remarkable—those who tirelessly pounded animal hides into supple leather to clothe their families; those who waited out blizzards in homesteader shacks; those who packed lunch pails for husbands headed to the mines and fields; those who started their own businesses to support their families; and those who built churches, schools, and libraries.

They were heroines who left their marks in many ways. They all helped make Colorado the special place it is today.

"AUNT CLARA" BROWN

(ca. 1803–1885)
ANGEL OF THE ROCKIES

Clara Brown, an African-American slave, watched in despair as her youngest daughter, Eliza Jane, climbed trembling onto the auction block. Clara wanted to comfort the frightened child, but she knew that disrupting the auction could prove calamitous for herself and her daughter. Besides, she was in no position to help. Her own turn on the block was only minutes away.

The sun burned as hot as a blister on that summer day in 1835, as the bidding began in the public square in Russellville, Kentucky. When it finally subsided, the auctioneer shouted his familiar refrain, "Going once, going twice, sold!"

Clara could hardly bear to watch as Eliza Jane, her face twisted with terror, was led away by her new owner. Clara didn't recognize the buyer, and she knew her daughter might be taken off to some distant place, never to be seen again. The same was likely to happen to her husband, Richard, and their two older children, Margaret and Richard Junior, who stood numbly nearby.

By day's end Clara's worst fears had been realized. Her husband and two older children had been sold and had disappeared from her life forever. But she never abandoned hope of finding them or her dear Eliza Jane.

Remarkably, Clara didn't become bitter over the breakup of her family or other indignities she suffered as a slave and a black woman.

"My little sufferings was nothing, honey," she told a reporter in 1885, "and the Lord He give me strength to bear up under them. I ain't complaining."

Clara Brown Denver Public Library, Western History Collection, Z-275

Instead, after winning her freedom in the late 1850s, she made her mark as Colorado's first black settler and a prosperous entrepreneur. She also devoted much of her time to helping the needy. Her fellow Coloradans called her their "angel of the Rockies"—high praise for someone who had so many hardships to overcome.

Clara was born in the slave quarters of a Tennessee plantation at the dawn of the nineteenth century. Sources variously claim her birth year as 1800 or 1803, and she herself couldn't remember the exact date during an 1885 interview. In that same interview, she told a reporter from the *Denver Tribune Republican* that her grandparents were American Indians.

"Thus her peculiar cast of face is accounted for," the reporter wrote. "It is wholly unlike the usual African type, and must impress all who study it with its singular strength."

When Clara was barely more than a toddler, she and her mother were sold to tobacco farmer Ambrose Smith. When Smith moved to Kentucky, strapping Clara went along to toil in the fields and clean and cook in the Smith home. Her days were dominated by drudgery and hard work, but religious revivals offered her some respite. One preacher in particular made an impression that changed Clara's life. According to biographer Kathleen Bruyn:

> So vividly did the young evangelist describe Jesus' agony that she then and there concluded that no sacrifice any human being could be called upon to make could compare with the voluntary suffering of the Son of God. Never in her life did Clara subscribe to the "hellfire and damnation" syndrome which ordinarily drove sinners to the mourners' bench. Compassion, not fear, motivated her all her life.

Clara married another slave named Richard, and together they had four children. One of them, Eliza Jane's twin sister, Paulina, drowned at a young age. The family faced a second calamity in 1835, when Ambrose Smith died and his heirs decided to sell his slaves to settle his debts. The decision ripped apart Clara's family like a hurricane leveling cotton.

If there was a bright spot in the devastating event, it was that Clara was purchased by George Brown, a merchant and friend of Ambrose Smith, who had a reputation for treating his slaves decently. Clara adopted his surname. When Brown died in 1857, he left a will that freed, or manumitted, her. By law, she had to leave Kentucky within a year if she were to retain her freedom, so she moved to St. Louis and then on to Leavenworth, Kansas.

Clara was content working as a domestic in Kansas, but she was unsettled by the debate raging there over whether slavery should be banned. Though free, she still feared slavery. Rumor had it that slave traders were kidnapping free blacks in Kansas and ferrying them to states where they could be sold as slaves.

Clara was intrigued by reports that blacks enjoyed more freedom on the western frontier. She also wondered whether members of her family might have taken refuge there.

In April 1859 Clara learned of a wagon train that was leaving shortly for Colorado. She asked if she could join the train as its cook in exchange for her fare. The organizers agreed.

Two months later, the sixty-wagon expedition arrived in Auraria, a scattering of cabins at the confluence of Cherry Creek and the South Platte River. Unlike most of the people swarming to Colorado, Clara did not suffer from gold fever, but she figured she could profit from those who did. She took a job at Auraria's City Bakery, where she cooked for prospectors and miners.

As she had hoped, Clara found greater acceptance in the West. Most of her customers and neighbors were friendly; they called her Aunt Clara or Aunty. When she befriended the Reverend Jacob Adriance, a Methodist minister to the homeless, she knew that he had barely enough food for himself, much less others. So she cooked extra helpings at dinnertime and delivered the food to the minister, claiming that she accidentally had cooked too much. It would be a sin to waste food, she told him, as she forced him to take it.

Clara also opened her own one-room cabin for prayer meetings, but most of the new settlers were more interested in gold than in God. As Clara listened to their tales of new ore discoveries in the mountains, she saw another opportunity. She moved to Central City to open a laundry, reported to be the state's first. She charged fifty cents to wash and press a bundle of clothes.

Clara's business was immediately popular. She wisely reinvested her earnings in mining claims and property and began to grubstake prospectors who were down on their luck. Some of her investments paid off handsomely. By the end of the Civil War, she had accumulated ten thousand dollars' worth of property, according to historian Jeanne Varnell.

"It was said that eventually she owned seven houses in Central City, sixteen lots in Denver, plus mines and properties in Georgetown, Boulder, and Idaho Springs," Varnell wrote.

What Clara didn't invest, she donated. She prepared meals for penniless miners and their families and cared for them when they were ill or injured.

"She was always the first to nurse a sick miner or the wife of one, and her deeds of charity were numerous," reported the *Denver Republican* in 1890.

Clara also loved to donate to church construction funds. She didn't care what the denomination was; she believed that God worked through many. The only time Clara pinched pennies was when it came to her own needs. She shunned fancy clothes and living quarters.

Clara did dip into her savings so she could visit Kentucky a decade or so after her departure. She went in hope of finding her husband and children, but after several weeks of searching, she failed to find any clues as to their whereabouts. She began to think that perhaps God wouldn't lead her to her family because He had other plans for her. Perhaps He wanted her to help some of the impoverished ex-slaves, including a nephew she had met on her visit to Kentucky.

The former slaves hadn't fought in the Civil War, but they were still among its victims. They could not get jobs because the war had devastated the nation's economy. Clara invited a number of former slaves to return with her to Colorado. She agreed to pay their way and house them temporarily, but they would be responsible for finding themselves jobs and permanent housing. When Clara returned, Colorado newspapers applauded her generosity.

But Clara refused to rest on such laurels. She knew she must work harder than ever to ensure the success of those she had sponsored. Doing so was getting more difficult; she was now in her late sixties, and she tired quickly. Her finances ailed as well. Her trip to Kentucky had eaten up her savings, and her investments had faltered. Floods had destroyed buildings she owned in Denver and washed away the records that proved her ownership of lots in the city. In 1873 a fire destroyed three buildings she owned in Central City. Then she was conned by crooks who realized that this trusting, illiterate black woman was an easy target.

Still, Clara's compassion did not die. She raised money to help former slaves known as Exodusters, who had fled to Kansas from the South in the late 1870s. These former slaves, who moved west following Reconstruction, called themselves Exodusters because they felt they were on an "exodus" or journey to freedom. Their plan was to form their own independent communities. The Exodusters had been freed by passage of the Thirteenth Amendment, but they continued to be exploited by white landowners. Thousands of Exodusters flocked to Kansas when they heard rumors that they could find free homestead land, farm equipment, and rations there. But for most, the stories were as illusory as a prairie mirage. They found no homes and little food in the so-called Promised Land.

Clara rushed to Kansas to distribute relief money that she had raised in Colorado. When she returned home in the fall of 1879, the *Central City Register* reported:

> *Aunt Clara Brown, whom everybody in Central knows, returned from a visit to Kansas some few days since, whither she went to look into the condition of the colored refugees and in the interest of the sufferers generally. There were about 5,000 all told, and they are getting on as fast as could be expected. The greater portion have found employment, and the balance will, doubtless, in the course of time. Aunt Clara says they are an industrious and sober class of people who only ask an opportunity to make an honest living. Their cry is work, work, and that is being given them as fast as possible. She was kindly received by [Kansas] Governor St. John and the people generally. She thinks that in another year these people will be well-to-do and self-supporting.*

Clara now tired even more quickly in the high mountain air, and she was troubled by edema. She had to rest in bed frequently. Alarmed friends urged her to move to Denver, where the lower altitude might help her to recuperate. An old friend, Denver Mayor Lee Sopris, arranged for her to live in a cottage rent free. Other friends delivered meals, and a doctor agreed to treat her at no charge.

By this time, Clara doubted she would ever see any of her family again. For years she had tried to locate someone who might know anything about her husband and children, but to no avail. Her efforts finally paid off in the spring of 1882 when an old friend wrote that a woman matching Eliza Jane's description was living in the Midwest. Though

Clara was close to eighty and in poor health, she was determined to investigate. Friends offered to pay for the trip.

According to one account, Clara took a train to Council Bluffs, Iowa, and was traveling through town by streetcar when she saw a familiar figure walking along the muddy street. She stepped off the streetcar and joyfully reunited with her daughter. She learned that Eliza Jane had married another slave, but he had disappeared during the war. Eliza Jane had raised five children on her own.

Clara returned to Denver accompanied by her daughter and a granddaughter. She felt at peace with the world, having fulfilled her lifelong dream of finding Eliza Jane. But while her spirit soared, her health worsened. On October 26, 1885, she died from congenital heart disease.

Clara's funeral drew mourners of all races who wanted to pay tribute to her spirit and good works. She died destitute, so the Colorado Pioneer Association paid for a burial plot at Riverside Cemetery in Denver. Later, a permanent chair was dedicated to her at the Central City Opera House. She was inducted into the Colorado Women's Hall of Fame and was memorialized with a stained-glass window at the Colorado Capitol.

These honors acknowledged Clara's role as one of the state's founders, as well as her devotion to helping others despite the many barriers she faced herself. As the Colorado Pioneer Association said, Clara was a "kind old friend whose heart always responded to the cry of distress, and who, rising from the humble position of slave to the angelic type of a noble woman, won our sympathy and commanded our respect."

ELSA JANE GUERIN

(Born ca. 1837)

MOUNTAIN CHARLEY

Fifteen-year-old Elsa Jane was playing with her two young children when she heard a knock on the door of her small St. Louis home. When she answered it, a somber messenger told her, "I have some bad news for you."

She knew immediately that the news must concern her husband, a Mississippi riverboat pilot. The messenger explained that he had been shot and killed by one of his mates, an ill-tempered fellow named Jamieson. Young Elsa Jane felt her world turn topsy-turvy. Where once life had "flowed on in quiet, uninterrupted beauty," she later recalled, now the future looked grim and ugly.

Not only had Elsa Jane lost a loving husband, but she had lost her sole source of support as well. She was estranged from her parents and couldn't rely on them for help. She knew she would have to go to work to support herself and her children, but she had never learned a trade.

"I knew how great are the prejudices to be overcome by any young woman who seeks to earn an honest livelihood by her own exertions," she later said.

In desperation, Elsa Jane devised a plan: She would disguise herself as a man to improve her chance of getting a job that paid a decent wage. From her perspective the plan offered another advantage. Disguised as a man, she might have a better chance of "some day returning upon Jamieson, with interest, the heavy misfortune he had visited" upon her. Jamieson had been convicted of her husband's murder and sent to prison, but he had been released on a technicality after serving little time.

Wracked with regret, Elsa Jane persuaded the Sisters of Charity to look after her two children. Then she dressed in men's clothing, spoke in a deep voice, and began cussing like a double-crossed cowboy.

"I buried my sex in my heart and roughened the surface so that the grave would not be discovered—as men on the plains cache some treasure and build a fire over the spot so that the charred embers may hide the secret," she said in an 1861 account of her adventures titled *Mountain Charley, or the Adventures of Mrs. E. J. Guerin Who Was Thirteen Years in Male Attire.*

Elsa Jane was soon hired on as a cabin boy on a steamer sailing between New Orleans and St. Louis. She earned thirty-five dollars a month, most of which she mailed to the Sisters of Charity for the support of her children. Once a month, she donned a dress and visited them. These happy occasions sometimes made her yearn for her former life, but she could never figure out how to resume the role of mother and yet earn enough money to support her family. Besides, she was discovering other benefits to being a man in a man's world. She wrote:

> *I began to rather like the freedom of my new character. I could go where I chose, do many things which while innocent in themselves, were debarred by propriety from association with the female sex. The change from the cumbersome, unhealthy attire of woman to the more convenient, healthy habiliments of a man, was in itself almost sufficient to compensate for its unwomanly character.*

For four years Elsa Jane hid her true identity. When her employer, the captain of the steamer, died, she went to work as a brakeman on the Illinois Central Railroad. She was soon forced to flee when a coworker discovered her secret.

Back in St. Louis, she prowled the boisterous saloons along the riverfront still dressed as a man. One night she spotted Jamieson and followed him down a dark street. She had promised herself that if she ever met him, she would "shoot him precisely as I would a mad dog."

Elsa Jane waited until no one else was nearby and then called out to Jamieson to stop. She told him why she had followed him and that she intended to send "his black soul to the devil who gave it." She fired her pistol at Jamieson, but the bullet missed its mark. He pulled out his pistol, but his shot went wild as well. Elsa Jane's second shot nicked Jamieson's shoulder. He screamed in pain, then squeezed off another shot and fled. Elsa Jane crumpled to the ground with a gaping wound in her thigh. She crawled down an alley and fainted.

A few hours later, a kind widow discovered Elsa Jane and took her into her home to recover. The leg took six months to heal. Meanwhile, Elsa Jane couldn't work, and she badly needed money. When neighbors told glittering stories of gold discoveries out West, she figured she had found an answer to her dilemma.

Elsa Jane joined an expedition of fortune seekers headed for California in 1855. There, she earned thirty thousand dollars running a saloon, hauling provisions to gold camps, and running a ranch before she returned to St. Louis to visit her children. But soon she "tired of the inactivity" of her life and "determined to seek adventure in some new direction." Colorado was experiencing its own gold rush, so she traveled there to work as a trader for the American Fur Company. Later, she opened a tavern in Denver called Mountain Boy's Saloon. Her customers, believing that she was a man, called her Mountain Charley.

Occasionally, Elsa Jane took time off from work to scout the countryside on a mule. One spring day in 1859, as she rode through a narrow gorge near Denver, she saw a rider approaching from the opposite direction. Even from a distance, he looked familiar. As Elsa Jane and the man drew closer, they recognized each other at almost the same instant. It was Jamieson, and he lunged for his gun as Elsa Jane did the same. Jamieson's bullet sailed harmlessly over Elsa Jane's head. Hers knocked Jamieson to the ground.

"I emptied my revolver upon him as he lay," Elsa Jane said in her book, "and should have done the same with its mate had not two hunters at the moment came upon the ground and prevented any further consummation of my designs."

The hunters built a litter to carry Jamieson back to Denver. He recovered from the three gunshot wounds Elsa Jane had inflicted, but he died soon after in New Orleans of yellow fever. Before he left the Denver area, Jamieson revealed Elsa Jane's secret to residents there. But he also insisted that she not be punished for shooting him. He explained that her attack was justified because he had killed her husband. Elsa Jane would not have to go to prison, but she could no longer pass herself off as a man.

Elsa Jane continued to dress in men's attire, though she no longer tried to act the part. In fact, she married H. L. Guerin, who had worked for her as a bartender. The couple sold the saloon in 1860 and moved to St. Joseph, Missouri.

There, Elsa Jane wrote her remarkable autobiography. Few copies of the book were published, so her tale was not widely circulated. In the beginning, the book reads like a romance novel, but the story rings more true in later chapters, such as one that describes a wagon trip out West. In Wyoming, she said, "mountains rise upon mountains till they seem to meet the sky, forming a scenery of the most majestic and beautiful character. Upon Independence Rock are cut and written the names of thousands of emigrants, and my own was added to the rest."

In the book's foreword, Elsa Jane assured readers that her account was "literal actual fact" except for some conversations and the details of a couple of dramatic scenes.

Was she telling the truth? Colorado historians Fred M. Mazzulla and William Kostka think so. In their introduction to a 1968 reprint of her book, Mazzulla and Kostka note that the Colorado places and details that Elsa Jane described did exist, and that Denver city records show there was a Mountain Boy's Saloon on Blake Street, one of the main business streets in 1860.

In 1859 the *Rocky Mountain News* featured an article on Mountain Charley and said her real name was Elsa Jane Forest. In the book Elsa Jane referred to herself as Mrs. F___ at the time of her first marriage. Other details in the article conform to those in the book, too: Elsa Jane's widowhood as a teenager, her life in St. Louis before adopting her disguise, and her trip to California.

Still, Mazzulla and Kostka concede that frustration awaits anyone who tries to confirm Elsa Jane's story. There are few accounts of her life aside from the book, and there are several reports of a Mountain Charley who did not fit Elsa Jane's description. General George West, publisher of the *Colorado Transcript* of Golden, wrote three articles in 1885 in which he said Mountain Charley had revealed her story to him in 1859 but made him promise not to publicize it for at least twenty-five years. The Charley he wrote about came from Iowa, married at eighteen, and was deserted by her husband shortly after she gave birth to a stillborn child. Dressed like a man, she followed her "dandified looking" husband and his "low-down" lover to Pikes Peak country in order to get revenge.

West's Charley was a Denver card dealer before enlisting in the Iowa Cavalry during the Civil War under the name Charles Hatfield. Dressed as a male soldier—something a handful of women actually did—she served with troops in Missouri. Her superiors occasionally asked her to spy on Confederate camps while in the garb of a woman. Two doctors discovered her true sex when she was wounded in the line of duty, but they agreed to keep her secret. This Charley was promoted to first lieutenant before the end of the war, and afterward she reportedly married and raised four children in Iowa. Another reporter for the Rocky Mountain News once described Mountain Charley as "the veritable and notorious Charley, smoking, drinking, swearing," and consorting with men.

The exact identity of Mountain Charley may never be known. Nonetheless, Elsa Jane Guerin's book offers a fascinating look at how one woman may have coped with the terrible hardships and heartaches that confronted members of her sex in the nineteenth century. As Mazzulla and Kostka say:

> *Whether Mountain Charley was one unique young woman or several interesting young ladies masquerading in men's clothing cannot be determined. Like Isabella Bird, the English gentlewoman in bloomers who climbed Longs Peak and rode alone through the Colorado wilderness, one or all of the Mountain Charleys were seeking freedom from the repressions of the Victorian Age.*

JULIA ARCHIBALD HOLMES

(1838–1887)

CONQUEROR OF PIKES PEAK

Julia Holmes's bloomers flapped like a flag in the brisk breeze as she scrambled over boulders and loose rock to reach the top of Pikes Peak. She panted to catch her breath in the thin mountain air. Every muscle ached, but she hardly noticed. Instead, she tingled with exhilaration, for she had just conquered one of Colorado's tallest peaks. Not only that, but she was the first known white woman—perhaps the first woman of any race—to reach the 14,110-foot summit.

Twenty-year-old Julia stood on top of the world and scanned the horizon—first west, then north, east, and south. Then she sat down on a rock to rest and record her thoughts on August 5, 1858:

> *I have accomplished the task which I marked out for myself, and now I feel amply repaid for all my toil and fatigue. Nearly every one tried to discourage me from attempting it, but I believed that I should succeed, and now, here I am, and I feel I would not have missed this glorious sight for anything at all. In all probability, I am the first woman who has ever stood upon the summit of this mountain, and gazed upon this wondrous scene. . . . How I sigh for a poet's power of description, so that I might give you some faint idea of the grandeur and beauty of this scene. Extending as far as the eye can reach, lie the great level plains, stretched out in all their verdure and beauty, while the winding of the grand Arkansas [River] is visible for many miles. We can also see distinctly where many of the smaller tributaries unite with it. Then the rugged rocks all around, and the almost endless succession of mountains*

Julia Archibald Holmes Denver Public Library, Western History Collection, F-7348

and rocks below, the broad blue sky over our heads, and seemingly
so very near—all, and everything, on which the eye can rest, fills
the mind with infinitude, and sends the soul to God.

When news of Julia's feat hit the newspapers, Americans were thrilled. Only half a century earlier, Lieutenant Zebulon Montgomery Pike had contended that no human being could ever reach the top of the daunting mountain that would come to bear his name. Now, a woman had done just that—and she had done it at a time when society frowned on members of the "weaker" sex engaging in such strenuous physical activity. Women were supposed to climb social ladders, not mountains. As one enlightened physician lamented in the late 1800s, "The active sports that make the brothers healthy and strong are not permitted the sisters, and yet without good reason."

Julia's accomplishment fueled a growing sentiment that women *could* excel at physical tasks, that they could overcome the same tough obstacles as men if only given the chance. As Colorado historian Marshall Sprague noted:

> *Historians have found in [Julia's climb] a sharp reminder that women in the West, as everywhere else, have always performed as well as men—women pioneering, suffering, challenging, creating, adapting, enduring. They have performed well even though their roles have been underplayed because of the custom, persistent until recent decades, of assigning to men alone most positions of leadership.*

If any woman was destined to conquer Pikes Peak, it was Julia Archibald Holmes. Born February 15, 1838, in Nova Scotia—the second of eight children—she was a headstrong child raised by parents who were willing to challenge the conventions of the day. Her parents, John and Jane Archibald, were ardent foes of slavery, and in 1848 they moved their family to Massachusetts, a hotbed of the abolitionist movement. Six years later, they joined reformers who flooded Kansas with the hope of keeping it a slave-free state.

These "Free State" sympathizers faced strong and sometimes violent opposition from pro-slavery forces, and clashes between the two groups were frequent. Tensions mounted even higher with the arrival in the state of the famous abolitionist John Brown, who believed in spilling blood, if necessary, to stop the "wicked, cruel, and unjust" institution of slavery. By 1856 Kansas was in a "state of open insurrection and rebellion," according to its acting governor.

James H. Holmes, of New York, was eager to help the cause. The daring young adventurer rode into Kansas and quickly fell under fiery John Brown's spell. When Brown asked him to investigate a report that pro-slavery thugs from Missouri had murdered Brown's son, Holmes tracked down the suspects and shot one of them.

But Holmes had a gentler side as well. During frequent visits to the Archibald home, which was a rendezvous for abolitionists and a station on the Underground Railroad, he was entranced by slender, handsome Julia and impressed by her courage and outspokenness. He proposed, and the couple married on October 9, 1857. Soon after, they decided to join friends from Lawrence, Kansas, who were headed to Colorado to search for gold. They were driven, Julia claimed, not so much by a desire to strike it rich as by "a desire to cross the plains and behold the great mountain chain of North America."

Julia packed her wedding finery and outfitted herself in bloomers: loose-fitting pantaloons covered by a short skirt. The garment was named for Amelia Bloomer, the militant editor of a temperance and women's rights journal, *The Lily*. In the early 1850s, bloomers were the rage among leaders of the women's suffrage movement, including Julia's mother. Wearing them constituted a form of political rebellion, but women also found them to be much more practical for outdoor wear than the voluminous and constraining dresses that were the fashion of the day. In bloomers it was much easier and more comfortable to ride horseback or hike rugged trails.

Traditionalists hated bloomers; they considered them scandalous and unladylike. Other members of Julia's Colorado expedition grumbled their disapproval when they saw her wearing them, but she was unfazed.

"I cannot afford to dress to please their taste," she said. "I couldn't positively enjoy a moment's happiness with long skirts on to confine me to the wagon."

Julia suspected that she was the first woman in bloomers to cross the prairie, a trip that took a month and covered about five hundred miles, most of it over the Santa Fe Trail. At one point, she wrote in her diary:

At first I could not walk over three or four miles without feeling quite weary, but by persevering and walking as far as I could every day, my capacity increased gradually, and in the course of a few weeks I could walk ten miles in the most sultry weather without being exhausted. Believing, as I do, in the right of woman to equal privileges with man, I think that when it is in our power we should, in order to promote our own independence, at least, be willing to share the hardships which commonly fall to the lot of man.

To show that she was in earnest, Julia startled the men by insisting that she take a turn guarding their camp at night. The guardmaster considered this an insult. Another member of the party, a man named W. J. Boyer, described brash Julia in a letter he sent to his family back home: "She's a regular woman's righter, wears the Bloomer, and was quite indignant when informed that she was not allowed to stand on guard. She is young, handsome, and intelligent."

And what did Julia think of the men who dismissed her notions of equal rights—and responsibilities—for women?

"Of such stuff are generally the croakers against reform everywhere," she said.

For the most part, though, members of the expedition had gold—not women's rights—on their minds as they set up camp near what is now Colorado Springs. They were eager to prospect, but because of their inexperience, they found little more than a few flakes of gold. As their dreams of a quick fortune faded, Julia and James began to ponder a different goal: the formidable mountain that loomed above their camp.

Lieutenant Pike had discovered Colorado's best-known peak while exploring the area in 1806. He dubbed it Grand Peak, but cartographers later changed the name to Pikes Peak in his honor. The explorer tried to climb the mountain but was thwarted by a late November storm, prompting him to say that "no human being could ever have ascended to its pinnacle."

Fourteen years later, Dr. Edwin James, a naturalist-historian with the Long expedition, did reach the top. And on August 1, 1858, Julia, James, and two other men began their ascent. Julia lugged a seventeen-pound backpack stuffed with bread, clothing, and a quilt to fend off the mountain chill, for even in August the party would encounter snow. She chose to wear her "American costume"—bloomers, moccasins, and a hat—so she could clamber more freely over rocks and snowbanks. The going was steep and tough; Julia often had to pull herself along by grabbing at branches and jutting stones. After two days of climbing, she wrote in her diary:

Down at the base of the mountain the corral of fifteen wagons, and as many tents scattered around it, form a white speck, which we can occasionally distinguish. We think our location grandly romantic. We are on the east side of the Peak, whose summit looming above our heads at an angle of forty-five degrees, is yet two miles away—towards the sky.

For the last leg of the climb, Julia's party carried only writing materials and a copy of Ralph Waldo Emerson's *Essays*. When the group reached the top, they scanned the horizon.

"It was cold and rather cloudy," Julia noted, "with squalls of snow, consequently our view was not so extensive as we had anticipated."

The climbers scratched their names into a large rock and listened as Julia read from Emerson. Their celebration ended when snow enveloped the peak, and they began their descent. In her letters and journals, Julia never mentioned any difficulties on the climb down, but another Kansan described in a letter a "serious accident, which happened to Mrs. Holmes on the mountain top, which so nearly cost her her life."

What, if anything, happened remains a mystery. Julia obviously suffered no injury serious enough to prevent her from returning to camp. Another mystery is whether Julia was the first woman to reach the top of Pikes Peak. Could an American Indian woman have preceded her? No one knows for sure.

Before the end of the nineteenth century, yet another woman would find fame at the top of Pikes Peak. Katherine Lee Bates, an author and teacher from Massachusetts, was able to ride to the summit in 1893 via covered wagon and mule. The Pikes Peak Carriage Road had opened only four years earlier. The view from the pinnacle inspired in Bates the "poet's power of description" that Julia had so yearned for. Shortly after her trip, Bates wrote the classic patriotic anthem "America the Beautiful," an eloquent description of the nation's heartland as seen from high "above the fruited plain."

Julia and the other Kansans remained in Colorado another month after her ascent, growing increasingly frustrated by their failure to find gold. With the arrival of autumn, some headed back to Kansas, and others trekked north to the Denver area. Julia and James decided to explore northern New Mexico, where they ended up living for several years. Julia taught school and worked as a correspondent for the *New*

York Herald Tribune, while James served for a time as secretary of the new territory.

While in New Mexico, James and Julia had four children, two of whom died in childhood. The couple left the territory in 1863 and eventually divorced. Julia settled permanently in Washington, DC, where she worked in various federal jobs. She also resumed work on reform issues, lobbying Congress to give women the right to vote and speaking at the first women's suffrage convention in Washington in 1869.

Whether Julia ever returned to Colorado is unclear, but members of her family lived there for many years. Her brothers, Ebenezer and Albert Archibald, built one of the first homes in Trinidad. Her son, Ernest Julio, and her mother were also longtime Colorado residents.

Julia died on January 19, 1887, at the age of forty-eight. Although she spent only a brief part of her life in the West, she nonetheless left her mark there. She demonstrated that pioneer women could overcome tremendous challenges and accomplish the seemingly impossible if given the chance. She also served as an example of the opportunities the West offered women to step outside society's conventions. In the words of Agnes Wright Spring, who collected Julia's letters and journal entries for a book entitled *A Bloomer Girl on Pike's Peak, 1858:*

> *[Julia] pioneered, not only in climbing Pike's Peak, but in wearing the reform dress, in defending equal rights, and in holding public office. She established a reputation as a poet and writer. Her name, though not accepted, was among those considered in 1899 for a portrait in Colorado's Capitol dome. Her accomplishments stand side by side with those of Susan B. Anthony, Ida Husted Harper, and other women pathbreakers.*

Frances Wisebart Jacobs

(1843–1892)

MOTHER OF CHARITIES

In the swarming slums and tenement districts of the late 1800s, tuberculosis spread like wildfire. Physicians had no medicine to cure it and were helpless to quell it. The best treatment they could offer TB patients was "climatic" therapy: Move to a higher elevation where the skies are sunny and the air is clean—a place where less pressure on delicate lungs might offer a better chance of healing.

For many tuberculosis sufferers—or consumptives, as they were commonly called—Colorado was just what the doctor ordered. By one estimate, a third of the state population suffered from TB in 1880. More than thirty thousand consumptives lived in Denver, earning it a reputation as the "World's Sanatorium." Yet the city had no treatment facilities, neither a hospital nor a sanatorium. And there were few other accommodations for the sick. Most TB victims lived in shacks, tents, or dilapidated houses with little more than a bedroll, a washstand, some eating utensils, and a few personal belongings.

Frances Wisebart Jacobs, a Jewish housewife who moved to Denver in 1870, became increasingly appalled as she walked the city streets and witnessed the suffering of the sick.

"Most of the Denver community ignored those who roamed the city coughing or hemorrhaging," she later recalled.

But Frances, a cheerful, big-boned woman with the energy of an army, was not one to ignore a need. In 1872 she helped organize the Hebrew Ladies' Benevolent Society. Two years later she founded the nonsectarian Denver Ladies' Relief Society. Both provided food, clothing, and other essentials to the city's neediest residents.

Frances Wisebart Jacobs History Colorado, Biographical Portrait File, Scan No. 10026350

Frances also did something few other Denverites were willing to do: She exposed herself to the highly contagious disease. She waded through ankle-deep mud and snow on the Platte River bottoms, delivering food, coal, and medical supplies to the hovels where the "lungers" and "coughers" lived. She also distributed bars of Grandpa's Tar Soap because she had never gone "anywhere where food was needed that soap was not needed worse." When Frances found a patient who needed immediate medical care but couldn't afford a doctor, she summoned her own physician and paid the fee from her purse.

Some Denver elites sniffed that Frances was "not fastidious . . . or particular in her tastes." But her friends knew the truth: Frances ignored the misery and grime because "her heart was too full and her hands too busy to permit any natural feeling of disgust," as one friend said. "The love that prompted the duty overpowered all other emotions. Her keen sense of humor was a great help to her. Her nature was sunny. She saw the bright side of everything."

Despite the grim and dreary circumstances in which she often worked, Frances also played a prominent role in Denver high society. She had a beautiful voice and was often invited to sing or recite poetry at public events. In 1881 she was a key organizer of a major Denver social event: a charity ball at the Tabor Opera House, built by Colorado silver millionaire Horace Tabor. Frances was among four hundred who danced the night away, looking resplendent in a "black satin de Lyon with a brocade velvet front, beautiful flora garniture and point lace."

In the late 1880s Frances conceded that Denver's TB problem was too big for her to conquer on her own. She began lobbying government leaders, businessmen, clergymen, and journalists to build a TB hospital. One day she marched into the newsroom of Denver's largest newspaper and demanded of the editor, "Why can't you start a movement to get a hospital big enough to take care of these people who walk the streets . . . ill unto death coughing away what little life is left? It is a reproach to the city and to all of us that when they fall on the street the police patrol comes, and the sick man is taken to jail. That is the terrible thing I have seen."

But city leaders balked. They feared a TB hospital would only lure more consumptives to Denver and damage the city's image. But Frances persisted, and finally she persuaded the Jewish community to build a medical center. Today the facility, known as National Jewish Health, is ranked as one of the world's premier respiratory treatment centers.

President Franklin D. Roosevelt once said of the facility, "The opportunity for health through this fine institution is outstanding, and those who are responsible for it may well feel that they are doing a work far beyond estimate in the ordinary terms of value."

Frances Wisebart Jacobs was born in Harrodsburg, Kentucky, on March 23, 1843. Her parents were immigrants from Bavaria. In 1859 one of her six siblings, Benjamin Wisebart, and a friend, Abraham Jacobs, went west to make their fortunes. They sold supplies to miners from a general store in Central City, Colorado. Abraham also ran a stage-coach south to Santa Fe, New Mexico.

In 1863 Abraham returned to Cincinnati, where the Wisebarts were then living, to marry Frances, his childhood friend. The couple returned to Central City and started a family. Of their three children, one died young. Their son Benjamin eventually became a lawyer, and daughter Evelyn became an educator. After seven years in Central City, the family moved to Denver, where Abraham ran another store.

While Abraham became active in local politics, Frances plunged into charity work. Not only did she organize the relief societies, but she also created Denver's first free kindergarten and joined forces with two local clergymen to form the Charity Organization Society, a model for what later became the United Way of America.

Frances also advocated women's suffrage and better conditions for young working women, including an eight-hour day, improved housing, and a reformed public employment office. She let Denver residents know that the employment office had sent girls to jobs that "ruined them for life." She complained that she had seen girls "of 12, 15 and up to 17 years of age, who knew more of the vices and immortality than I may tell you of in a lifetime."

Frances's efforts sprang from her belief that everyone was part of the fellowship of man and thus had a responsibility to help the less fortunate, even those of another faith. At a Denver conference on charity issues, she declared, "How are you to have that sympathy for the poor, miserable creatures whom you meet? It is only by having a oneness with man and God." Because of her remarkable success at creating Colorado charities—and her dynamic speaking skills—she was often invited to address national conferences of the Association of Charities and Corrections.

Despite her message of compassion, Frances didn't believe in coddling those unwilling to help themselves. When she encountered a family that was destitute due to the father's laziness, she didn't spare the man a tongue-lashing. As a friend, Samuel Eliot, once said:

> She told the truth about the actual, but always held up the hope of the possible. She possessed that rare balance of firmness and gentleness which is the mark of a strong, broad, deep nature. She could be serene when serenity was the truest kindness. She could be gentle and comforting where sympathy was needed. She possessed indomitable patience, so that she was never weary in well-doing, and her physical strength was remarkable. Her feet were always swift on mercy's errands, her head was busy with wise designs, her hands were always ready for service, her heart was overflowing with love.

Frances's devotion to helping others was even more remarkable given the many blows her own family suffered: the death of a son, a fire that destroyed Abraham's business in Central City, and the failure of Abraham's clothing store in Denver in 1885.

Perhaps her charity work was one way of trying to salve her own wounds. But at the same time, she helped heal countless others, especially through the hospital she inspired.

Although Frances initially couldn't persuade city leaders to build the TB hospital, she found an ally in a new rabbi at Temple Emanuel, William S. Friedman. He preached in favor of a Jewish-sponsored hospital so fervently that, in 1890, the city's Jewish Hospital Association was incorporated. Construction on the new hospital began that October.

Ironically, Frances fell ill and never saw her dream fully realized. Instead of following her doctor's advice to stay home and recuperate, she continued to walk city streets ministering to the sick. She was only forty-nine when she died of peritonitis in the spring of 1892.

Two memorial services were held for the woman the press heralded as Denver's "mother" or "queen" of charities. More than two thousand mourners attended the first service at Temple Emanuel, presided over by Rabbi Friedman and three leading Christian clergymen. The second service at the First Congregational Church included speeches by the Colorado governor and Denver mayor.

In recognition of Frances's work, the Jewish Hospital Association trustees voted to name the new hospital after her. Construction was completed in 1893, but the nationwide Silver Panic dried up financing and kept the hospital standing empty for six years. The national B'nai B'rith decided that it was the responsibility of all American Jews to support the hospital. The organization began soliciting money from across the country, enabling the facility to open in 1899. Although the facility was renamed the National Jewish Hospital, it was nondenominational and open to anyone in need. Its motto: "None may enter who can pay, and none can pay who enter." Denver's *Rocky Mountain News* editorialized:

It consummates the work begun years ago by one of Denver's noble pioneer women, Mrs. Frances Jacobs, but on a broader and more extended scale than she had planned. . . . While the "Frances Jacobs Hospital" will not exist in name, it will be a pleasure to know that out of her efforts has grown an institution, national in its scope, and dedicated to the humane and charitable work in which during her lifetime she so earnestly engaged.

More than a century later, tuberculosis has become a relatively rare disease due to advancements in the field of medicine. The hospital that Frances envisioned deserves part of the credit. As of 2010, National Jewish Health (the current name of the facility) had been named the top respiratory hospital in the nation for thirteen consecutive years by *U.S. News & World Report*. It is also rated one of the top biomedical research centers in the world and has been instrumental in developing more effective asthma medications.

Not only is Frances immortalized in the bricks and mortar of National Jewish Health, but she also is the only woman among sixteen pioneers honored with stained-glass portraits in the rotunda of the Colorado Capitol in Denver.

After her death, a fellow charity worker, the Reverend Myron Reed, marveled at all that Frances accomplished:

I think of her as I saw her not long ago walking in the mud and under the rain to visit an unfortunate. She had seen, face to face, more people in trouble than anyone in Denver. Under the load of other people's troubles she walked these streets as long as she could. . . . I observed that she kept the law, "Bear ye one another's burdens," and the other law, "Bear your own." Doing this kind of work she was about the most cheerful woman I remember, the most undisturbed. I always thought of her as being planned [sic] to control affairs—to do large things in a large way. No one thinks of anyone to fill her place.

CHIPETA

(1843–1924)

INDIAN PEACEMAKER

Ouray, the charismatic chief of the Ute Indians, did not realize the danger he faced as he traveled to the Los Pinos Indian Agency in 1872. The federal government had officially recognized him as the leader of the Utes, but some tribal members resented his authority and blamed him when the government broke its treaty promises. Five Utes had hatched a plot to murder Ouray when he reached the agency in southwestern Colorado.

At the last minute, the conspirators had a change of heart—except for a warrior named Sapovanero, who happened to be the stepbrother of Ouray's wife, Chipeta. As Ouray hitched his horse to a post at the agency, Sapovanero lunged from a hiding spot, brandishing an ax. Ouray sensed that something was wrong and jumped aside just as his brother-in-law swung the ax at his head.

Ouray tackled Sapovanero and grabbed him by the throat, but before he could take his revenge, Chipeta snatched Ouray's knife from its scabbard and out of his reach. Her quick reflexes saved her stepbrother's life. More important, she averted a calamitous split among the Ute leaders. The incident was one of many in her lifetime that demonstrated her courage and commitment to peace.

"Chipeta was well thought of by her own people and was always allowed and often especially invited to take part in the council meetings—no other Ute woman . . . was ever so allowed," wrote Albert B. Reagan and Wallace Stark, government agents who worked with the Utes in the early 1900s.

Chipeta was born June 10, 1843, to Kiowa Apache parents who were killed by Indian raiders when she was still a baby. A band of Tabeguache Utes found her crawling around her parents' ransacked camp.

Chipeta History Colorado, Biographical Portrait File

They raised her and named her Chipeta, which has been translated both as "White Singing Bird" and "The Charitable One."

Ouray was one of the Utes' most respected hunters and warriors. When his first wife died in 1859, Chipeta began caring for his son, Paron. She quickly impressed Ouray with her intelligence and beauty. Ouray, who was twenty-six, asked Chipeta, then sixteen, to marry him. According to historian P. David Smith:

> *She was a typical Ute wife of the time: hard-working, shy, quiet, and the person who did almost all of the day-to-day household tasks, which would have included tanning Ouray's deerskins and elkskins to use for sewing his clothes and moccasins; cooking, including preparing dried meats; hauling wood; and carrying water. Chipeta helped raise Paron and loved him as her own child.*

Chipeta was as devastated as Ouray when Sioux warriors raided their hunting camp north of Denver in 1863 and kidnapped Paron. The Sioux later gave the boy to a group of Arapahoes, traditional enemies of the Utes. Chipeta and Ouray spent years fruitlessly searching for him. Federal officials once tried to exploit Ouray's concern for Paron by promising to find and return him if Ouray complied with their treaty demands, but father and son were never reunited.

Although Ouray and Chipeta had no children of their own, they adopted three young Utes. By tribal custom, Ouray could have married another woman who could bear him children, but he refused to do so out of love for Chipeta.

When gold was discovered near Pikes Peak in 1859, white prospectors and settlers flooded Colorado. Confrontations between them and the native tribes escalated. When Indians were shot without provocation, some Utes wanted to retaliate.

Ouray had already distinguished himself as a skilled hunter and ferocious warrior, but he realized that the Utes could never drive off the settlers. There were simply too many of them. He advised his people to try to live alongside the whites and negotiate treaties that would preserve their way of life. As a result, he became known as the Peace Chief.

One early settler in northwestern Colorado, David S. Gray, remembered an occasion during his childhood when he met Ouray face to face. A group of Indians had surrounded the Gray family's new home one day in the late 1870s, and Gray and his siblings panicked and fled. One of the Indians raced after them on horseback and assured the children that they were in no danger.

"He spoke excellent English and seemed much disturbed at having caused so much excitement," Gray later recalled. "That party was Chief Ouray and his family. We saw many Indians in the years that followed. They were always friendly and very hungry."

Ouray had no close male friends. He preferred to spend time with Chipeta, despite the commonly held Ute belief that women were inferior to men and should be ignored as much as possible. Chipeta had the respect of other Utes, too, because of her beauty, intelligence, and bearing. Some of the Indian agents referred to her as the "Queen of the Utes."

Chipeta actively supported her husband's peace policies. She lobbied other tribal leaders and joined Ouray on trips to Washington, DC, to discuss treaties with federal officials. On one such trip in 1880, "Chipeta, with her native charm and dignity, became the darling of Washington society," according to author Jeanne Varnell. "She was dressed in Victorian finery and was given valuable gifts of silk dresses, millinery, gloves, and silver pieces for her home."

Colorado newspaper editor Caroline N. Churchill reported at the time that Chipeta's "appearance was so picturesque as to teach a national lesson, that beauty or style need not be confined exclusively to any one portion of the race."

When frontier explorer Ernest Ingersoll met Chipeta in 1874, he found her "about the most prepossessing Indian woman" he had ever seen. "Ouray was immensely proud of her."

Chipeta and Ouray eventually settled on a productive three-hundred-acre farm on the western slopes of the Colorado Rockies. Federal agents deeded the farm to Ouray and agreed to pay him one thousand dollars in return for his willingness to work with them as chief of the Utes. Over the years, Ouray, who spoke several languages, negotiated treaties that guaranteed specific lands for Utes in return for other land and government aid.

To encourage assimilation, Ouray and Chipeta donned whites' clothing, adopted their customs, and entertained white friends at their sixteen-room adobe house. Chipeta served meals on fine china and entertained by playing guitar and singing.

But the couple's comfortable lives were shattered in 1879 when White River Utes rebelled against Nathan Meeker, a misguided Indian agent who was trying to force them to cease their nomadic ways and become farmers and ranchers. The angry Utes slaughtered Meeker and twenty-nine other men. They also kidnapped three white women, including Meeker's wife and daughter. When Ouray intervened, the warriors agreed to release the women. Nonetheless, whites around the country were outraged when they learned that the Meeker women had been raped. They paid scant attention to the Meeker women's statements that Ouray and Chipeta had treated them with kindness.

"We were given the whole house, and found carpets on the floor, lamps on the tables and a stove with a fire brightly burning," Meeker's daughter, Josephine, later wrote. "Mrs. Ouray shed tears over us."

In the wake of the Meeker Massacre, white settlers demanded that the federal government remove the Utes from Colorado. Despite Ouray's efforts to reestablish peace, in 1880 officials canceled the Utes' treaty rights to their twelve-million-acre homeland on Colorado's western slopes and prepared to move them to a new reservation on a barren tract of land in eastern Utah.

Ouray continued to urge the Utes to live peacefully with whites. In 1880, at the age of forty-seven, he died while on a treaty mission near Durango. With his death Chipeta lost her influence. When a white settler wanted her farm in 1881, she was forced to leave it. She joined 1,400 other Utes on a forced march to a reservation on Bitter Creek in Utah. Officials promised her a new home as nice as her old one, but she was given an unfurnished two-room place with unplastered walls. Outside, there was no water to irrigate crops.

A Denver newspaper reported that Chipeta married a sheepherder named "Toomuchagut." But given the unlikeliness of the name, some people suspected that the story was concocted to belittle the Utes.

What historians do know is that Chipeta, disillusioned by the government's treatment of her people, eventually abandoned any vestige of white culture and reverted to the nomadic Indian life she had known as a child. Her days in Utah were filled with indignities. Once, in 1887, armed white men rode into her camp while she was gathering food with other Ute women. The men threatened to rape them, then burned the camp to the ground when Chipeta helped the women escape.

As Chipeta got older, she reverted to living in a tepee. She was nearly blind with cataracts and suffered from rheumatism. In 1916, when she was seventy-three, a sympathetic Indian Affairs official visited her at Bitter Creek to see if he could do anything for her. She replied, "I desire nothing; what is good enough for my people is good enough for me. And I expect to die very soon."

But Chipeta lived on for eight more years. She died on August 17, 1924, and was buried in a ravine near Utah's Book Cliffs. The following year, when friends worried that her remains might wash away in a flash flood, they reburied her near her old farm a couple of miles south of Montrose. More than five thousand people formed a procession a mile long as they came to pay tribute to her memory. The honor contrasted starkly with the last days of her life, when she had lived in near anonymity. Finally, Coloradans had recognized the important role she played in western history.

Today the nine-acre historic site where Chipeta is buried—Chief Ouray Memorial Park—features her large granite crypt, a tall stone monument to Ouray, and the Ute Indian Museum, which recently was renovated and expanded.

"It is somehow fitting that Colorado's largest and finest tribute to any Indian or Indian tribe is located at this spot—a spot first given to Ouray and Chipeta, then taken away from them, and finally dedicated to their memory," said historian Smith.

In a more poetic tribute, Colorado writer Eugene Field wrote almost a century ago:

But give her a page in history, too,
Tho' she be rotting in humble shrouds,
And write on the whitest of God's white clouds
Chipeta's name in eternal blue.

BLANDINA SEGALE

(1850–1941)
SISTER OF CHARITY

Friends had warned Sister Blandina Segale to steer clear of cowboys. But there was little she could do one night in 1872 when a lanky man in a broad-brimmed hat boarded the stage in which she was traveling. She sat paralyzed by fear as the coach jolted along a washboard road headed for Trinidad, Colorado. Later, she admitted:

> By descriptions I had read I knew he was a cowboy! With crushing vividness—"No virtuous woman is safe near a cowboy" came to me. I made an act of contrition—concentrated my thoughts on the presence of God—thought of the Archbishop's blessing, "Angels guard your steps," and moved to such position as would put my heart in range with his revolver. I expected he would speak—I answer—he fire. The agony endured cannot be written. The silence and suspense unimaginable.

Finally, the cowboy did speak.

"Would you take a part of my kiver?" he drawled.

Before she could answer, the man tossed half of his buffalo robe onto her lap to ward off the winter chill. Then, sizing up her voluminous black habit, he asked, "What kind of lady be you?"

She mustered the courage to speak: "A Sister of Charity."

"Whose sister?"

"Everyone's sister, a person who gives her life to do good to others."

"Quaker-like, I reckon?"

"No, not quite."

Sister Blandina Segale Sisters of Charity of Cincinnati

Sister Blandina soon realized that she had misjudged the young man. She set aside her preconceived notions and began quizzing him about his background. In the course of their conversation, she learned that he had run away from home six years earlier to become a cowboy, and he hadn't written to or visited his mother since. The nun made the young cowboy promise to write home as soon as he reached his destination.

That night, Sister Blandina learned that the myths of the West didn't always reflect reality. She also discovered that even hardened cowhands could benefit from her moral guidance. The Catholic nun put those lessons to good use during the next two decades as she served her faith in Colorado and New Mexico. She became a major civilizing force in the Southwest, and the results of her work can still be seen today. She built schools and hospitals, spoke out against racism, helped the disabled and the poor, and persuaded Indians and whites to settle their differences peacefully. She even talked Billy the Kid out of murdering four Colorado doctors.

Years later, when the tireless and selfless sister sailed to Rome to seek sainthood for another nun, Alfred Segal of the *Cincinnati Post* wrote:

People say that Sister Blandina is saint enough herself, canonized by sixty years of faithful doing. Trinidad, Colorado, knew her for a saint sixty years ago when she went there to teach. And if Trinidad was a rough place when she entered it, gentler it was when she departed. Rude men reverenced her walking among them as she did, unafraid; she offered a holy presence by which the power of pistols was shamed.

From infancy Sister Blandina had seemed destined to serve God. She was born Maria Rosa Segale on January 23, 1850, in northern Italy. After her baptism, her mother carried her to a mountain sanctuary and prayed that she would someday "comfort the sorrowful . . . harbor the harborless . . . visit the sick [and] teach [God's] ways to mankind."

When Maria Rosa was four, the Segales moved to America and settled in Cincinnati, a hilly city that reminded them of Italy. The family of six lived in a crowded one-room apartment, and Maria Rosa and her siblings attended a Catholic school. There, they experienced firsthand the good works of the Sisters of Charity. Maria Rosa soon realized that she wanted to be a nun.

At the age of sixteen, she entered the Sisters of Charity motherhouse in Cincinnati, adopting the name Sister Blandina. Her beloved older sister Maria Maddalena joined her and became Sister Justina. The two, though close companions, eventually were separated for several decades as each followed her calling, but they stayed in close touch through letters. Sister Blandina also kept extensive journals while serving in the Southwest. These were published in 1932 as a book titled *At the End of the Santa Fe Trail.*

The book offers a remarkable glimpse into the lives of the Catholic priests, friars, and nuns who helped to tame the Wild West. In it, Sister Blandina emphasized her courage and action rather than her fears and failures. Perhaps she was thinking of those readers who might follow in her footsteps. She didn't want to discourage them from ministering in the West.

Sister Blandina was only twenty-two years old when she got her orders to leave Ohio for missionary work in Trinidad. At first, she believed she was headed for an island in the West Indies, but she emerged from her stagecoach on December 9, 1872, in Trinidad, Colorado Territory— a rowdy mining camp with just two dusty streets, each about two blocks long. Only one of the local houses resembled any of the homes she had known back in Cincinnati; most were nothing more than ramshackle huts shoddily constructed of mud and wood. They looked, she thought, like kennels for dogs.

According to popular lore, the town of Trinidad was named either for the Hispanic lover of one of the town's founders or for the Holy Trinity. No doubt Sister Blandina preferred to believe the latter.

The people of Trinidad seemed friendly enough, but tension lurked beneath the community's surface. Rumor had it that renegade Ute Indians might attack the settlement to avenge the encroachment of whites on their traditional homeland.

There were other threats to Trinidad's tranquility as well. Because it was located only twelve miles from the New Mexico border, the town served as a rendezvous for outlaws fleeing from one territory to another. Scofflaws knew that in Trinidad justice was anything but swift and sure. They could burrow out of jail long before the circuit judge arrived from Denver.

Like others on the frontier, Trinidad residents sometimes took the law into their own hands. Soon after Sister Blandina's arrival, an elderly couple was murdered, and a posse quickly captured and hanged four Mexicans for the crime. Two days later, several white men who'd been arrested on other charges admitted that they had killed the couple.

Sister Blandina realized how impossible it would be to eradicate violence and "undesirable conditions" in the West. It would be, she later said, like "attempting to stop an avalanche." But she also knew that she had to try. For inspiration she turned to her church, her fellow sisters, her neighbors, and the stunning landscape all around her. Soon after she arrived in Trinidad, she wrote:

> *Here, if you have a largeness of vision, you find the opportunity to exercise it; if a cramped one, the immense expanse of the plains, the solid Rockies, the purity of the atmosphere, the faultlessness of the canopy above, will stretch the mind toward the Good. . . . I wish I had many hands and feet, and a world full of hearts to place at the service of the Eternal. So much one sees to be done,*

and so few to do it. I have adopted this plan: Do whatever presents itself, and never omit anything because of hardship or repugnance.

One of the first problems Sister Blandina addressed was the dilapidated building that housed Trinidad's Catholic school. Her order couldn't afford to build a new schoolhouse, so Sister Blandina devised an ingenious plan. She would climb onto the roof of the building and start tearing it apart with a crowbar. An incredulous friend asked how wrecking the building would accomplish anything. Blandina's reply reflected her faith in human nature: "The first good Mexican who sees me will ask, 'What are you doing, Sister?'" she explained. "I will answer, 'Tumbling down this structure to rebuild it before the opening of the fall term of school.'" The townspeople, she knew, would not let her toil alone.

She was right. No sooner had she started to rip away the roof than men began arriving with tools and building materials. In several weeks she and other townsfolk had erected a roomier, brighter, and better-ventilated schoolhouse.

Sister Blandina similarly used her wits—and her courage—to solve other dilemmas. One day a frightened student told her that his father had been arrested for shooting another man. A mob milled outside the jail, preparing to hang the prisoner if his victim died of his wounds. Sister Blandina decided to visit the victim and ask if he would forgive his attacker on the condition that the attacker be prosecuted. The victim agreed.

Sister Blandina asked the sheriff to escort the prisoner to the wounded man's bedside. The sheriff feared that a mob would try to kidnap the prisoner, but Sister Blandina argued that he would be safe if she accompanied them. The sheriff relented and took the accused man to the room where his victim lay dying. Sister Blandina made sure that the door was open so the crowd outside could hear the conversation between the two men.

"My boy, I did not know what I was doing," the repentant prisoner told his victim. "Forgive me."

The wounded man responded by pulling aside his blanket to reveal his grotesquely injured leg.

"I forgive you," he said, "as I hope to be forgiven, but the law must take its course."

"Yes, the law must take its course—not mob law," Sister Blandina repeated loudly so that the gathering outside could hear.

The mollified crowd dissipated. Sister Blandina had saved the prisoner's life, though he would still serve ten years in prison. Her lesson in forgiveness put an end to lynch mobs in Trinidad.

Sister Blandina tried to help other men deemed incorrigible by society. She once got word that a member of Billy the Kid's gang was wounded and dying in an abandoned hut. She brought him food, water, and bedding and continued to care for him even after he confessed to robbing and killing travelers along the Santa Fe Trail. The man warned her that Billy the Kid planned to kill Trinidad's four physicians for refusing to treat his wounds.

The nun came to the hut one day and found that the dying man had visitors. One of them, a teenager with a peachy complexion and steel-blue eyes, introduced himself as Mr. Chism. Sister Blandina realized that he was William Bonney, the infamous Billy the Kid.

"We are all glad to see you, Sister," Billy said, "and I want to say, it would give me pleasure to be able to do you any favor."

"There is a favor you can grant me," Sister Blandina replied.

"The favor is granted."

"I understand you have come to scalp our Trinidad physicians, which act I ask you to cancel."

Billy hesitated but remained true to his word.

"I granted the favor before I knew what it was, and it stands. Not only that, Sister, but at any time my pals and I can serve you, you will find us ready."

A year later, Billy encountered Sister Blandina again when he ambushed a stagecoach. When he saw that the nun was among the passengers, he rode away without robbing them.

In 1881 Sister Blandina returned Billy's good deeds by visiting him in a Santa Fe jail. Cautious guards had cuffed the young desperado's hands and feet and locked him to the floor, but they hadn't bowed Billy's spirit.

"I'll get out of this; you will see, Sister," he said.

He was right. He eventually escaped after killing two guards—only to meet his end a few months later at the hands of Sheriff Pat Garrett.

Sister Blandina had mixed feelings about Billy the Kid. She believed he had qualities that could have made him great, but he had squelched them to become an outlaw. In her journal she lamented the death of "poor, poor" Billy. Yet she also acknowledged that he was the "greatest murderer of the Southwest." According to legend, Billy had murdered twenty-one people by the time he was age twenty-one. The actual figure is probably less. Sister Blandina once waxed philosophical about the infamous outlaw: "Life is a mystery. What of the human heart? A compound of goodness and wickedness. Who has ever solved the secret to its working? I thought: One moment diabolical, the next angelical."

Sister Blandina had many other encounters with violence in the West. In 1883 she had to abort a trip to the San Bernardino Mountains because of a risk of attack by Apache Indians. The Indians were enraged because a white man had shot a tribal member without provocation. Now a group of them, armed with guns and bows and arrows and smeared with red and yellow war paint, sat on horseback on a knoll not far from the railroad camp where the nun had stopped on her journey.

Sister Blandina offered to try to negotiate with the Apaches. Praying and fingering her crucifix, she walked slowly toward them.

"My teeth began to chatter and my knees to knock against each other," she later wrote, "but my brain worked fast." She thought she might be able to calm the angry warriors because she had once tried to establish a school for their children.

She convinced the Apaches that the killer was not at the camp, and they decided to search elsewhere. Sister Blandina then suggested to the camp leader that he send out word that the murderer should be turned over to the Apaches. She realized that this was probably a death sentence, but the gesture could prevent the slaughter of many other innocent white settlers. She told the camp leader:

It is plain that, unless the Apaches are pacified, they will break from their reservation and then who can hold Geronimo and his band. [In the future] please do not mention this incident to me, or what became of the man. The advice to turn the murderer over to the Apaches is given, as my conscience dictates. I'm not certain that theology bears me out.

This was one of the few times that Sister Blandina confessed to being uncertain about her actions. However, she was certain about the need to remedy the many injustices that pervaded the frontier— including those perpetrated against American Indians. She often spoke out against racism—an uncommon sentiment for the period— and objected to efforts by whites to exterminate Indians and steal their land. Once an Indian chief approached her at a railway station and asked her about establishing schools for his tribe's children. The local Indian agent, who was standing nearby, asked if she felt oppressed by the chief's presence. She retorted, "The oppression just now comes from another quarter."

Sister Blandina considered federal Indian policy to be as insensitive as that agent. She once wrote:

> *Poor, poor Indians! They are doomed to lose. Then will come strict adherence to reservation rules—then diminution of numbers, and then extinction. Often have I pondered over the amount of money expended by our government to civilize the Red Man, and how ineffectually that money has been expended.*

Sister Blandina saw many other injustices and problems that she felt required her personal attention. Anyone in need could count on her assistance, and her energy seemed boundless.

"I do not know what fatigue feels like," she once said. "It is stimulating to meet emergencies."

Indeed, during her twenty-one years in Colorado and New Mexico, she accomplished more than most people could in a lifetime. Besides building Mount San Rafael School in Trinidad, she spearheaded the construction of St. Vincent Hospital in Santa Fe and a convent, St. Vincent Academy, and San Felipe School in Albuquerque. Sister Blandina Convent still stands adjacent to the San Felipe de Neri Church, the oldest Catholic parish in Albuquerque. The academy was later razed to make way for a bank, but the school building still stands and now houses a museum in Albuquerque's Old Town. St. Vincent Hospital still serves the sick and injured of Santa Fe.

After almost a dozen years in Santa Fe and Albuquerque, Sister Blandina returned to Trinidad in 1889. She found that the tiny town had "lost its frontier aspect." Inmates could no longer easily dig themselves out of jail, and Billy the Kid was nothing more than a legend.

"The remaining men who were ready at the least provocation or no provocation—except that of strong drink—to raise the trigger have settled down to domestic infelicity," she observed.

Sister Blandina returned to teaching. She also raised money to run Trinidad's new Mount San Rafael Hospital, which still exists today. But while she had overcome countless obstacles before, she now encountered one she couldn't surmount. In 1892 the Trinidad school board asked her to stop wearing her black nun's habit to class. The board said it was "inappropriate" for a public school and "brings us into trouble."

Rather than abandon her habit, Sister Blandina left Trinidad to become principal of St. Patrick School in Pueblo. In her book she expressed her disappointment over the turn of events in Trinidad: "Adios, Trinidad, of heart-pains and consolations!"

A year later, in 1894, Sister Blandina returned to Cincinnati. She was sorry to leave the West but glad to return home and be reunited with her sister. A few years later, she and Sister Justina founded the Santa Maria Institute to help immigrant Italians. They ran it together for thirty-five years.

"They offered shelter to women stranded and without work; gave food to hungry men and found them jobs; guarded the children of working women in their day nursery; visited homes; looked after erring children; visited prisons," said the *Cincinnati Post*.

The need was so great that the institute eventually expanded to four buildings. Still going strong, it recently celebrated its one hundredth anniversary and moved into even larger headquarters.

Somehow, indefatigable Sister Blandina found time to help in other ways. She became such a fixture in juvenile court that city officials made her a probation officer. She also led campaigns to rid Cincinnati of prostitution and white slavery.

In 1931, when she was eighty-one, Sister Blandina sailed to Rome to ask the pope to confer sainthood on Mother Elizabeth Seton, who had founded the American Sisters of Charity and the nation's first parochial school. Sister Blandina's friends thought she was equally deserving of sainthood. Though she never achieved that status, her work has been recognized in many ways. In 1958, for example, Regis College of Denver awarded her its Civis Princeps (First Citizen) Award in education. Sister Blandina has even been honored in Italy, where the town of Cicagna, where she was born, named a public square after her in 1998.

Sister Blandina didn't slow down until she retired from the Santa Maria Institute in 1933. Then she returned to her motherhouse and devoted her days to praying, writing, and listening to political and religious radio broadcasts. After she fell and broke a hip in 1937, she was bedridden for almost a year, but she refused to complain. When visitors asked if she needed help, she would reply, "No, child, not for me, but for God." Then she would add, "He must be very pleased with you, child. Always keep your chin up, and your eyes on God."

Sister Blandina died on February 23, 1941, a month after celebrating her ninety-first birthday. Her death was mourned from Albuquerque to Italy by the many people who had experienced her good works or been influenced by her guidance. They surely would have agreed with Sister Therese Martin, who once wrote of the kindly nun:

Failure never claimed her; discouragement never daunted the flashing, dark eyed, little figure. In spite of the flagrant spread of evil in the Territory, she carried on courageously, even gaily.

Sister Blandina never slackened in her struggle for perfection. She tried without ceasing to bring people so close to God that they would not even wish to offend Him by sinning. "To teach and meet emergencies as I see them," was her motto.

Mary Elitch Long

(1856–1936)

FIRST LADY OF FUN

Mary Elitch woke to a downpour on May 1, 1890. Her heart dropped. Today was to be the grand opening of Elitch's Zoological Gardens, a sixteen-acre amusement park near Denver that she and her husband, John, had labored for months to create. All that effort—and thousands of dollars of their own money—was in jeopardy. Why would anyone want to visit the park on such a dreary day?

"I was filled with grief and disappointment," Mary later remembered. "Mr. Elitch was nearly as sorrowful as I, for we had made great preparations for the opening and it seemed doomed to dismal failure. Looking back through the vista of years, I am sure my sorrow was for him far more than for myself. I remember I prayed very fervently for a cessation of those May showers."

To the couple's relief, her prayers were answered. As the sun climbed higher, the clouds lifted, and a messenger galloped to the gate of the resort to announce that a train filled to capacity was on its way from Denver. Moreover, he reported, roads to the Gardens were clogged with carriages, wagons, bicycles, and pedestrians. Mary was elated when the train huffed to a stop at the Gardens.

"How those people rushed the gates!" she recalled. "It certainly looked as if the entire population of Denver had accepted our invitation" to visit.

Throughout the summer, visitors continued to flock to Elitch's Gardens. By Labor Day, when the park closed for the season, John and Mary had made a jaw-dropping profit of thirty-five thousand dollars. But they still weren't satisfied that they had enough money

Mary Elitch Long History Colorado, Biographical Portrait File, Scan No. 10029205

to survive the lean winter months. So John decided to take the park's minstrel show on a tour of the Pacific Coast while Mary remained in Denver. When word arrived in February that John had pneumonia, she rushed to California. She was by his side when he died on March 10, 1891.

A widow at thirty-four, Mary not only had lost her beloved husband, but now she also faced the daunting decision of what to do with the Gardens. If she kept them open, she would need financial backers, since all of the Gardens' profits had been used to fund the minstrel show. Yet raising money would be a formidable task. The business world was a man's world. Mary would have to break new ground in more ways than one. If she were to continue to own and operate the amusement park, she would be the first woman in the world to do so.

"I determined to make these Gardens famous as a memorial to my husband," she said later. "My husband's death left our Gardens in my inexperienced hands. Our great adventure was still something of an experiment. I decided to undertake the management of the place myself, and so for the next twenty-six years, I operated the resort alone. It was a heavy burden."

To solve her cash-flow problem, Mary sold most of her own stock in the Gardens to local investors. But she stayed on as manager, and under her guidance Elitch's Gardens became so profitable that she was able to buy back all of the stock within three years. She even came to regard her gender as an advantage. "That Elitch's Gardens was conducted by a woman served as an attraction in itself to visitors," she said.

Mary plowed her profits back into the Gardens, believing that improvements and novel amusements would keep her customers coming back. She added moving pictures, a repertory theater, concerts, a ballroom, daredevil acts, amusement rides, and more. Her park became famous for providing high-quality entertainment for families at a relatively low cost.

A prominent civic leader, Father William O'Ryan, once gushed:

The Gardens are indeed a place of recreation for the people of the city, unusual and unique. There is nothing exactly like them in the whole country. Though public, welcoming every decent citizen, they seem something private, the joy and personal possession of each individual, a "garden enclosed," a place for quiet confidences and smiling meditations and personal joyance. . . . The gay laughter of little children, the voice of men and women, the whisper of young and old lovers, seem to hold in the Gardens the music of sincerity and holiness which are the essence of all true joy.

As founder of the Gardens—and an icon of Denver's cultural life— Mary had traveled far from her roots. She was born Mary Hauck in 1856 in Philadelphia. Within a few years, she moved with her family to California. There, as a teenager, she met John Elitch Jr., a large, athletic charmer six years her senior. He so swept her off her feet that she agreed to elope with him at the age of sixteen.

The couple moved to Denver in 1882 to begin building a life together. For several years they operated a restaurant called Elitch Palace Dining Room, cooking meals for miners, travelers, and some of Colorado's most prominent citizens. They bought a farm five miles northwest of Denver so they could grow fruits and vegetables to enhance their menu.

But they had another motive for buying the farm. Since visiting the Cincinnati zoo as a boy, John had dreamed of owning a zoo. And he and Mary fondly recalled the times they'd spent strolling through Woodward Gardens, a popular family attraction in San Francisco. Why not create something similar, they thought, for one of the fastest-growing cities in the Rockies?

Mary, a tall, slender woman with a perpetual smile, took on the task of designing the gardens, walkways, and fountains. John built enclosures for the zoo animals, many of which had already been donated by two friends who owned circuses; one of them was P. T. Barnum. The Elitches also erected a band shell, a vaudeville tent, benches, picnic tables, and a baseball field.

On opening day, P. T. Barnum, renowned circus dwarf General Tom Thumb, and other dignitaries joined the Elitches in launching their endeavor. Denver Mayor Wolff Londoner welcomed visitors, saying, "Denver has been longing for a place where a working man and his family can come and spend the day . . . where no lady will be offended by a disorderly person."

Mary never stopped expanding and improving the park. In mid-1891 she completed a playhouse that offered vaudeville and light opera. Soon afterward she added the West's first moving pictures, employing a flickering Thomas Edison Vitascope projector. She also hired a daredevil to parachute 1,500 feet from the basket of a gas-filled balloon. Young couples flocked to the Gardens to be married in the balloon as it floated high over the Gardens.

Mary was particularly fond of the animals in her zoo. A British journalist described her in 1898 as "the sole proprietor and manager of what is undoubtedly the finest zoological garden of its kind west of the Atlantic; and she can lay claim to the title of being the only woman in the world who possesses and manages a public zoo." He added that Mary owned "practically every animal except a giraffe and a hippopotamus."

Mary personally fed and trained many of her animals, including the lions and bears. Once, as thirty workers were digging a new bear pit, a large bruin escaped its nearby cage. Mary grabbed a broom and shooed the animal back into the cage as the frightened laborers scattered.

On another sunny day, hundreds of picnickers at the Gardens suddenly realized they were surrounded by dozens of slithering snakes. The reptiles, none of them poisonous, had escaped from a smooth-sided pit nearby. The zookeeper apparently had forgotten to feed them, and they were lured by the smell of food. Mary later recalled:

> *With wild shrieks the picnickers scrambled to their feet; abandoning the wonderful food that had caused the snake raid, they dashed madly off in every direction—upsetting other picnickers in their rush to safety. Some of the bravest set to and killed a number of the reptiles before the keeper and gardeners could catch and restore them to the pit, with a plentiful supply of food and precautions against another break for liberty. Peace was restored, extra food supplied, and the "victims" hailed as heroes and heroines forever after.*

Mary exploited her animals' antics—and displayed a Barnum-like flair for advertising—as she promoted her Gardens' wonders. A typical ad declared:

> *Come see the bears stand up and beg for peanuts; the monkeys slide down their toboggan slides, and the fierce billy goat engage in deadly conflict with the sacred bull of India. . . . And the baby lions—why, they're a whole zoological park in themselves.*

Mary's penchant for promotion helped steer the Gardens through tough times, including the Silver Panic of 1893, when a third of Denver's workers lost their jobs. Crowds still flocked to Elitch's Gardens, seeking an escape from their financial worries. Mary kept the Gardens family-friendly by banning liquor and rowdies. One writer noted that within the Gardens, "vulgarity and coarseness and loud shouts of the crowd need not the admonition of the policemen."

Although Mary never had children of her own, she delighted in watching them enjoy her amusements. She started a "free day" for children from nearby orphanages. Later she created Children's Day on Tuesdays, when parents could drop off their kids for a free day of tours, dance lessons, folklore, penny arcade games, carousel rides, and mile-long jaunts on a miniature train. Often as many as three thousand children swarmed the Gardens on Tuesdays.

In the evenings, many families came for the fireworks that spattered the skies like impressionistic paintings. One of Mary's assistants kept inventing new—and more powerful—pyrotechnics. The crowds showed their appreciation with gleeful "oohs" and "ahhs." Some of Mary's neighbors were less enthused; they visited her office the day after a particularly potent fireworks shows with bills for their shattered windows.

By the turn of the twentieth century, the Gardens were not just an amusement park, but the center of Denver's theater scene, thanks to Mary's decision to form the country's first summer stock company in 1897. In the winter, after the Gardens closed for the season, Mary would travel to New York City to recruit actors for the following year. She lured many legends to her stage, including Myrna Loy, Edward G. Robinson, Vincent Price, Gloria Swanson, Ginger Rogers, Lana Turner, and Sarah Bernhardt. She even launched the careers of some well-known stars. One lad became so fascinated with Mary's productions that he offered to scrub the stage in exchange for a ticket. Then he persuaded a director to give him bit roles in plays. When the boy, Douglas Fairbanks, earned fame as a film star, he always credited Mary's theater for launching his career.

"While the rest of the country has been in the theatrical dumps, the city of Denver has been the bright spot on the map," wrote a theater critic for the *Chicago Tribune* in 1900, when Elitch's theater could seat 2,500 people. In 1905 movie mogul Cecil B. DeMille played the Elitch theater and called it "one of the cradles of American drama."

Mary also enlivened the Gardens with music. In the early years, brass bands paraded around the grounds like peacocks. Later Mary hired symphony orchestras to play concerts. In 1917 she opened the Trocadero Ballroom and provided a venue for the nation's best big-band leaders, including Tommy and Jimmy Dorsey and Duke Ellington. Any young man wanting to impress a date made sure to escort her to the "Troc."

In 1900 Mary married her longtime assistant, Thomas Long, but he died only six years later, when his new car plunged off a mountain road. Once more Mary was left to run the Gardens on her own.

Over time the park began to struggle financially, in part because of Mary's generosity to Denver's charitable causes. Mary sold the Gardens to John Mulvihill in 1916, with the stipulation that she live rent-free in her fairy-tale cottage near the theater and get fifty dollars a month for the rest of her life. When the cottage began to deteriorate, Mulvihill built her a new brick home. Mary spent the last four years of her life living with relatives. She died at age eighty on July 16, 1936.

After Mary's death, her legacy lived on. While her zoo closed near the time of her death, the curtains didn't drop on Elitch's internationally renowned theater and concert performances until decades later. The rest of the amusement park, including an updated version of its famous Mr. Twister roller coaster, relocated to downtown Denver in 1994 and was still operating as of summer 2011.

Meanwhile, the original Elitch Gardens site has become a residential district known as Highlands' Garden Village. Only two structures remain from Mary's days: the 1891 theater and the 1926 carousel pavilion, which in 2009 was the site of a farmers' market and various community events. A local civic group hoped to raise $14 million to reconstruct the theater, the "grand dame" of Colorado performance stages, but as of 2010 it had not yet reached its goal. The original theater still stands after 120 years, as enduring as Mary's spirit.

For more than a century, tourists flocked to Elitch's Gardens to relax, play, and be entertained. As one advertisement for the Gardens boasted, "To not see Elitch's is to not see Denver."

Winifred Black, a columnist for the Hearst news syndicate, once said of the Gardens and their founder:

> *I'd cross the continent to spend a starlit, perfumed evening there with the apple trees, the birds and the people, the music and Mary Elitch, that rose of the world—that splendid, big-hearted, calm-browed mother of a woman, You can get all the grass and flowers and the trees together, but you haven't got the Rocky Mountains for a background, or the Colorado air of a medium to look through; and most of all, you haven't got our Mary Elitch or anyone like her.*

FLORENCE SABIN

(1871–1953)

DISTINGUISHED SCIENTIST

Five-year-old Florence Sabin was touring a Denver school with her mother when she noticed a group of students drinking from a wooden pail. As each child finished sipping water from the ladle, he or she handed it to the next person waiting in line. Florence, thirsty from walking, tugged at her mother.

"I want a drink, too," she said.

"No," her mother firmly replied. "All your life I want you to remember not to drink out of anyone else's cup, no matter how clean it looks."

Florence was puzzled by her mother's warning, but for the rest of her life she remembered what she later described as that "first lesson in good public health practices." It was the first of many lessons she learned on the way to becoming one of the nation's leading health researchers and teachers.

Florence reached the top of her profession despite many barriers that stood in the way of women interested in science and medicine. She became the first woman elected to the National Academy of Sciences, the first female full professor at one of the nation's top medical schools, and the first female president of the American Association of Anatomists.

Yet, despite her groundbreaking accomplishments, Florence remained a modest woman who preferred the anonymity of her laboratory and classroom to the public stage. She sought neither fame nor fortune but toiled to find a way to improve the human condition.

"A time will come when men and women will live their allotted span quietly, peacefully, without illness, free from pain, until they pass gently, as a tired child closes sleepy eyes, from this world to the next," she once said, voicing the goal to which she devoted her life.

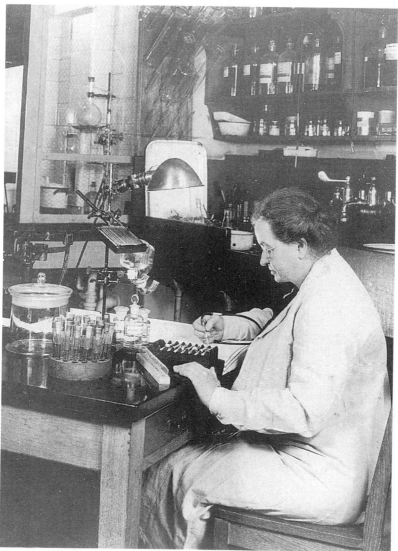

Florence Sabin Denver Public Library, Western History Collection, F-21153

Even after her retirement from teaching and research in 1938, Florence couldn't resist getting involved in efforts to improve Colorado's public health system. She lobbied for some of the nation's strongest public health laws, thereby enabling many Coloradans to lead longer and healthier lives.

Dr. Alfred Cohn of the Rockefeller Institute once said of Florence:

How came you to possess these many skills and virtues? . . . It has been, I think, because of your great humanity. You have cared deeply for your kind. And men have come to recognize in you that rare total person—of wisdom and of sentiment—heart and mind in just and balanced union.

Florence became that "rare total person" in spite of—or perhaps because of—a sorrowful childhood. She was born in Central City, Colorado, on November 9, 1871, one of two daughters of George and Serena Sabin. Two younger brothers died in infancy, and her mother died on Florence's seventh birthday.

Her father, a mine superintendent, felt incapable of caring for his two young girls, so he enrolled them in a Denver boarding school. Eventually, they were hustled off to live with relatives in Chicago and then Vermont. It was while attending the Vermont Academy, a fine girls' school, that Florence first developed her love of science.

In 1889 Florence joined her older sister, Mary, at Smith College—one of the few institutions of higher learning in the nation that accepted women. Always painfully shy, Florence buried herself in her books and avoided socializing. When she looked in the mirror, she saw a homely girl with frizzy hair and squinty eyes. She doubted any man would ever want to marry her, so she committed herself to building a career.

Science, especially medicine, was the subject that intrigued her most. She had relatives who were doctors, and her father had dreamed of becoming one, too. But she knew society had trouble accepting female physicians. There was a practical problem, too: Few medical schools admitted women students.

Still, Florence was inspired by the idea of becoming a doctor. Sitting at her dormitory desk, she absently scribbled on a piece of paper: "Florence Sabin, M.D. . . . Dr. Florence Sabin . . . Dr. Florence . . ." She liked the ring of it.

But soon another barrier threw itself in her path. Her father's health failed and his mining ventures faltered. He could no longer afford to pay Florence's tuition, so she took a job teaching at a Denver boarding school for two years and then returned to Smith College as an assistant instructor. She scrimped and saved every penny she could.

During Florence's junior year at Smith, she learned that Johns Hopkins University in Baltimore was opening a new medical school. Three wealthy women had pledged money toward its construction, but only on the condition that women be admitted on the same basis as men. In 1896 Florence was among the first sixteen women to take advantage of this opportunity. She excelled despite a daunting schedule that included embryology, physiology, and physiological chemistry. She particularly liked histology and anatomy, which were taught by a brilliant professor, Franklin P. Mall. According to Mary Kay Phelan, author of *Probing the Unknown: The Story of Florence Sabin:*

> *Early in her Hopkins career she heard [Mall] quoted as having said that from among ten thousand students, there might be one thousand who were highly intelligent. Out of this thousand perhaps five would start in research. All five could prepare specimens but only one would become a trained investigator. Already Florence's interest in research was stimulated. If only she could be that one in ten thousand.*

Florence soon demonstrated that she had the aptitude. In her second year she published a research paper titled "On the Anatomical Relations of the Nuclei of Reception of the Cochlear and Vestibular Nerves." Doing so was a rare honor for such a young student. Clearly, here was a budding scientist of abundant promise.

By her third year Florence was caring for patients. During her fourth year she delivered nine babies, some of them in shacks with no indoor plumbing. She preferred the quiet of a laboratory to the chaos of doctoring under such primitive conditions. So when Dr. Mall asked her to build a model of a newborn's brain stem, she jumped at the chance. No one had ever built such a model, and she was flattered to be given a task of such great significance.

Florence devoted every spare moment to the project. First she carefully dissected a brain stem. Then she used her observations to produce a three-dimensional model. When doctors studied the finished product, they were stunned to find that Florence had uncovered new information about the structure of the human brain.

In 1900 Florence graduated from Johns Hopkins and began her medical internship. At the same time, she continued her research and wrote about her findings. Her book, *Atlas of the Medulla and Mid-brain*, was for years considered the most authoritative text on brain stems.

Florence's friends encouraged her to become a practicing physician, but she was happier conducting research.

"All good laboratory workers are good cooks," she told them. "And I like to cook."

Eventually, Florence shifted her inquiries to the lymphatic system, which plays a critical role in the immune system by circulating body fluids that nourish and cleanse cells. She read all that she could on the topic—much of it in German—and then outlined the experiments she needed to reach her goals. Her research showed that lymphatic vessels develop from layers of cells in special fetal veins. This finding proved earlier theories wrong—and earned her a $1,000 award for the best scientific thesis written by a woman.

More important, Florence's breakthroughs were shattering the widespread belief that women lacked the drive, patience, and intellectual capacity to be good researchers.

"When the results of Florence's work became known, she was acknowledged as one of the first pioneers in proving that women can do work of the same caliber as men," according to biographer Phelan.

Florence's accuracy and originality contributed to her growing reputation as a top-notch researcher. As she squinted into a microscope, she kept her eyes open to new ideas. She would not be bound by conventional wisdom. She also wasn't afraid of being wrong and once wrote:

The investigator who holds back his conclusions until he is absolutely sure, never progresses far. When I reach certain conclusions, I do not hesitate to publish them, even though after further study, I may find I was wrong; then I do not hesitate to say that I have changed my mind.

As Florence's star rose, Johns Hopkins officials decided to break with tradition. They allowed Dr. Mall to add a woman—Florence—to the staff of his anatomy department. Florence was thrilled. She could now support herself doing something she really loved.

Of course, mankind benefited, too. Florence was destined to make more valuable discoveries, including the role of white blood cells called monocytes in defending the body against infection. She also developed a method that allowed her to study living cells through a microscope. Researchers everywhere eventually adopted her technique.

In 1905 Florence was promoted to associate professor of anatomy, the university's first full-time female faculty member. Other academic honors and speaking engagements from around the world soon followed.

When Mall died in 1917, Florence had all the credentials necessary to replace him as head of the department. But university officials balked at giving the job to a woman, even one as accomplished as she. They played it safe and hired a man.

Florence's feminist friends and pupils were outraged, but she ignored their entreaties to resign in protest.

"I'll stay, of course," she told them. "I have research in progress."

Johns Hopkins did offer her something of a consolation prize—she was promoted to full professor, another first for a woman at the medical school.

As a teacher, Florence influenced a new generation of researchers and doctors. From 1902 to 1925 all the freshman medical students at Johns Hopkins were required to take her anatomy course. They found her to be a tough taskmaster. She insisted that her students check and recheck all observations and discover answers independently. When one young man kept pestering her in class with questions about obscure topics, Florence soon realized that he was trying to fritter away time to prevent her from giving the next day's assignment. The next time he asked a question, Florence assigned him to find the answer in a two-volume textbook written in German. He was to report to the class on his findings the next day.

Despite her no-nonsense approach, Florence developed lifelong friendships with students and colleagues, shedding her shyness as her confidence grew. She loved to host dinner parties, and invitations to them were prized because she was such a good cook and conversationalist. She enjoyed inviting a mélange of guests—lawyers, writers, artists, musicians, students, and professors—and assigning them sides in debates on world affairs, art, literature, and politics. One of her guests was Gertrude Stein, who flunked out of medical school but made quite a name for herself as a writer.

Florence's parties gave people a chance to see a more intimate side of her.

"She developed a rare kind of affection, which was never imprisoning or demanding, but always left people free," said Dr. Lawrence Kubie, a student who became an internationally famous psychiatrist. "Everyone who touched her life felt this. . . . To them all she brought affection, simplicity and a spirit of unassuming and irrepressible youthfulness."

Some of Florence's best friends were suffragettes. She did her bit for women's rights by marching in parades, writing for feminist publications, and eventually becoming chairwoman of the National Women's Party. She also actively urged young women to consider careers in science.

"It matters little whether men or women have the more brains; all we women need to do to exert our proper influence is just to use all the brains we have," she once said.

Despite her long association with Johns Hopkins, Florence couldn't pass up an offer in 1925 to create a new department of cellular studies at New York City's Rockefeller Institute, the world's preeminent research facility. Over the next thirteen years, she supervised eleven research projects, some of which led to key discoveries about the causes and characteristics of tuberculosis, one of the world's leading killers.

Florence also championed the Gotham Hospital Plan, an endowment designed to help impoverished women pay their hospital bills. She didn't succeed in implementing the plan, but it did serve as a model for subsequent hospital insurance programs.

Florence continued to win accolades for her pathbreaking work. In 1929 *Pictorial Review* magazine awarded her five thousand dollars for the "most distinctive contribution made by an American woman to American life in the fields of art, science and letters." President Herbert Hoover invited her to the White House. *Good Housekeeping* named her one of the twelve greatest living American women, choosing her over Jane Addams and Helen Keller. Fifteen colleges awarded her honorary degrees. In 1951 her home state named a building on the University of Colorado campus after her, and eight years later it made her the subject of one of two statues representing Colorado in the US Capitol Statuary Hall.

Dr. Simon Flexner, director of the Rockefeller Institute, once described her as "the greatest living woman scientist and one of the foremost scientists of all time."

Florence had certainly earned the right to retire in 1938. At the age of sixty-seven, she returned to Colorado to live quietly with her sister. But when residents discovered the famous doctor in their midst, they asked her to help fix the state's ailing public health system. It was a huge task. Colorado had one of the worst public health records in the nation. The state spent less than most on public health despite having abysmal death rates due to disease and infant mortality.

"We think of our state as a health resort, but we're dying faster than people in most states," Florence contended.

At the age of seventy-three, Florence crisscrossed the state, investigating its public health problems and campaigning for more funding and new health laws to replace those enacted six decades earlier. She forcefully lobbied the state's movers and shakers. One senator later remembered being accosted in a drugstore by "this little bump of a woman with a twinkly sort of smile that made her eyeglasses seem to light up."

Florence's health agenda dominated the 1946 election in Colorado. When the newly elected governor was asked how he planned to get the program through the legislature, he replied, "I'll have the little old lady on my side. There isn't a man in the legislature who wants to tangle with her. She's an atom bomb. She's a dynamo."

In fact Florence succeeded in getting most of her legislative agenda passed. The "Sabin Health Laws" became national models.

Next, Florence turned her attention to health issues in Denver. She became the city manager of health and charities and pressed for better sewage disposal, garbage collection, rat reduction, restaurant sanitation, and tuberculosis treatment. Within two years Denver's death rate plunged to half of what it had been before her tenure. Florence donated her salary to medical research.

Florence finally retired from public service—this time for good—in 1951, so she could stay home and care for her ailing sister, Mary. Florence herself was seventy-nine.

"She had by then accomplished more for health in Denver than had been accomplished in all the city's previous history," said Colorado historian Hope Stoddard.

At the age of eighty-one, Florence's own health began to fail. She entered the hospital with pneumonia and, while watching her beloved Brooklyn Dodgers play in the World Series on October 3, 1953, she suffered a fatal heart attack during the seventh-inning stretch.

More than half a century later, Florence is still revered in Colorado. She reached the pinnacle of the science, teaching, and public health professions, and her work improved the lives of countless people. All of this she accomplished in the face of personal adversity and professional barriers. As writer Genevieve Parkhurst said in *Pictorial Review:*

> *Only by a complete devotion to her work has Dr. Sabin come to her large place in the world of science. Although she puts aside with a smile any hint that her way was not always easy, those who have followed her career closely, as associates and friends, declare that being a woman set many obstacles in her path. Wherever she triumphed it was by harder work and under greater difficulties then men would have encountered in the same circumstances. But she, herself, was never concerned with gaining credit. Her one desire was to make the best contribution she could toward easing humanity's pain.*

MARTHA MAXWELL

(1831–1881)

NATURALIST AND TAXIDERMIST

"Where did you get those buffaloes and bears?" "How do you stuff and mount something so big?" "Did you shoot them?" "Where are the bullet holes?"

Questions flew as visitors to the 1876 Centennial Exposition in Philadelphia marveled at a lifelike display of mounted animals: bears and buffalo, elk and antelope, beavers and mountain lions, ducks and eagles. The creatures seemed frozen in time, standing, crouching, and leaping across a simulated landscape that might have been carved right out of the western plains and mountains.

A sign beside the exhibit described it as "Woman's Work," and Martha Maxwell, the woman in question, did her best to answer the never-ending barrage of queries from the crowd jammed against the railing in front of her display. Later recognized as the first taxidermist ever to place her specimens in realistic poses and settings, she offered visitors from eastern cities a glimpse into an unknown world.

"Woman's Work" proved to be one of the most popular exhibits at the Centennial Exposition, an event described by one author as "a kaleidoscope of wonders, a complex mixture of patriotism and celebration that was the event of a lifetime for all who were a part of it." One reporter likened Maxwell to Diana, the Roman goddess of the hunt, and gushed that she was the most "observed" of all the exhibitors. Another wrote that her collection "induced many who otherwise would not have gone, to make the journey" to Philadelphia.

The exhibit clearly proved that Martha, a Colorado naturalist, deserved recognition as one of the country's leading authorities in

Martha Maxwell History Colorado, Biographical Portrait File

taxidermy, museum display, and natural history. But the event did not set Martha on the road to financial security, as she had hoped it would. Nor did it help to heal deep wounds that had developed in her personal life. When Martha died only five years later, in 1881, she was a lonely, despondent, and impoverished woman.

Martha's life was never easy. She was born in Pennsylvania on July 21, 1831. Her father, Spencer Dartt, died only two years later of scarlet fever. Her mother, Amy Sanford Dartt, was an invalid, so Martha was raised much of the time by relatives. Her free-spirited grandmother, Abigail Sanford, often took her on rambles through the Pennsylvania woods, and these outings planted the seeds of what would prove to be a lifelong passion for nature.

In 1841 Martha's mother married Josiah Dartt, a first cousin of Martha's late father. Josiah was a loving stepfather who encouraged Martha's thirst for knowledge. A devout Christian, he dreamed of ministering to Indians in Oregon. So the family packed its belongings and, in September 1844, set out by wagon for the Oregon Trail. They planned to winter in northern Illinois near the homes of Martha's uncles and complete the journey the following spring.

But a debilitating illness struck the Dartt family that winter, forcing them to abandon their ambitious travel plans. Instead, they moved to Baraboo, Wisconsin, where one of Martha's uncles had established a general mercantile. Josiah was hired on as a store clerk, a menial job that barely allowed him to support his family, which by this time included two more daughters, Mary and Sarah.

Josiah strongly believed in the lifelong pursuit of learning. He had an extensive library and expected, he once said, "to all eternity to continue to expand in intellect & increase in useful knowledge." He soon tired of shopkeeping and turned instead to surveying, which more fully engaged his mind. In his leisure time he read avidly, everything from Greek and Roman lexicons to the *New York Tribune,* and he encouraged his daughters to stretch their minds by engaging them in intellectual discourse. Despite his meager salary, he insisted on sending Martha to Oberlin College in Ohio, one of the few institutions of higher learning that accepted female students.

Martha loved Oberlin—the classes, the teachers, the social life, and the intellectual stimulation—but her tuition and living expenses became too great a financial burden for her stepfather to bear. She dropped out in 1852, a year after she had started.

Back in Wisconsin, she took a job as a schoolteacher, hoping to both further her own education and earn a living. Several months later, a prominent Baraboo businessman, James A. Maxwell, offered her a position as companion and chaperone for his two oldest children. Much to Martha's delight, he paid for all three of them to attend Lawrence College in nearby Appleton, Wisconsin.

It soon became apparent that James, a recent widower, saw in Martha something more than a governess. Not long after arriving in Appleton, she received a lengthy letter in which he proposed marriage.

"I like you, not because I think you handsome, above many," he wrote, "neither because I think you have gifts or graces, natural or acquired above many, but because I think you have good, warm affections with a sound judgment and discretion, to govern you in their direction and bestowment."

Martha was surprised by the proposal and apprehensive about accepting. She was only twenty-two; he was almost twice as old. She worried that she would be burdened with the responsibility of looking after his six children, and she wondered whether the two of them could be happy together.

"Matrimony, my dear girl, is a duet," he told her, "in which there is always more or less discord, at least until the parties learn to harmonize, until the characters modulate themselves to each other."

Apparently his arguments and assurances were persuasive. Martha set aside her misgivings, and the couple married on March 30, 1854. Three years later, Martha gave birth to her only child, Mabel.

As Martha had feared, she was nearly overwhelmed by domestic chores, but she refused to abandon her fervor for causes that had stirred her interest. She campaigned for women's rights, promoted the abolition of slavery, and railed against the evils of smoking and drinking. She even joined dozens of other women who stole out of their homes one night and raided several taverns, smashing bottles of liquor and letting them drain onto the floor. Martha and five other ringleaders of what became known as the "Whiskey War of 1854" were hauled into court and fined.

Trouble soon brewed at home, too. James's business ventures began to collapse in the Panic of 1857, and creditors seized some of his properties. Just when the family's financial situation seemed bleakest, James learned of the gold discoveries near Pikes Peak and of the feverish exodus of fortune seekers to Colorado Territory. In the spring of 1860, he and Martha packed their belongings into a covered wagon and headed west. Considering Mabel too young to make the journey, they left the two-year-old behind in the care of Martha's sisters and mother. The distance between mother and daughter would never entirely be erased.

The Maxwells arrived in the Central City mining district in May 1860. James spent most of his time prospecting, and Martha did her part to help support the family by opening a restaurant and washing clothes for miners. She earned enough gold dust to buy a ranch near Denver and more than twenty mining claims, none of which panned out.

On a visit to her new ranch, Martha was startled to find a German taxidermist squatting on her property. She went to confront him at his cabin and was intrigued by the feathered mounts he kept there. She realized they combined two of her favorite interests: art and natural history. When a court ordered the claim jumper off her land, Martha raided the cabin and eagerly carried off his specimens, hoping to figure out how they were constructed. As she examined each one carefully, her fascination with taxidermy blossomed.

In the fall of 1862, Martha returned to Wisconsin to visit her mother, who was seriously ill, and her daughter, whom she had not seen for almost three years. But five-year-old Mabel no longer recognized Martha. As far as the child was concerned, grandmother Amy was her mother.

For the next several years, Martha remained in Wisconsin caring for relatives. During her stay she enrolled in a nearby college to study natural history and taxidermy. She also joined several organizations involved in promoting progressive reforms. When the strain of her heavy schedule began to wear on her, she checked herself into a sanitarium for a rest. Then she moved to Vineland, New Jersey, which promoted itself as an idyllic community where people could live in harmony with nature and with each other.

Martha loved Vineland; her neighbors shared her passion for feminism and other progressive reforms. But James Maxwell was lonely, and he wrote urging her to come home to Colorado. She ignored his entreaties until 1868, when he traveled to New Jersey and pleaded his case in person.

Reluctantly, Martha returned with Mabel and James to Colorado, and the family settled in Boulder, then a town of about three hundred residents. Overwhelmed by the bounteous wildlife at the foot of the Rocky Mountains, Martha began to accompany her husband on hunting trips so she could observe animals in their natural habitats. She memorized every detail, hoping to reproduce them accurately later. James was an accomplished marksman, and he taught her to hunt and shoot as well as he did. Soon she was bagging many specimens herself.

When she wasn't hunting, Martha worked long hours on her mounts, experimenting with new tools and techniques. Most of what she learned she taught herself by trial and error. First, she would skin an animal. Then she would take measurements of the body and build an accurate model over which she could stretch the skin. At first she made her models from clay or plaster. Later, she fashioned them from light iron rods swathed in wool, cotton, or other materials. The only bones she used from the animals were the leg bones. As Maxine Benson pointed out in her biography *Martha Maxwell, Rocky Mountain Naturalist:*

> *Martha was thus using procedures in the late 1860s and early 1870s that were similar in principle to those that William Hornaday, the most celebrated taxidermist of the late nineteenth century, would develop a few years later. What is noteworthy about Martha's work is not the fact that a woman was mounting a variety of animals, large and small, but that anyone was employing such relatively sophisticated techniques in an isolated settlement at the edge of the Rocky Mountains in Colorado Territory.*

Martha went to great lengths to get the animal specimens she desired. Once when James shot a hawk, she climbed a large cottonwood tree in her dress to retrieve two chicks from its nest. Martha raised the birds until they were bigger and then euthanized them with chloroform. She mounted the baby hawks with their necks stretched upward and mouths gaping open. Suspended above them was their mother, gripping a rabbit in her talons.

Martha eventually had mounts of 47 species of mammals and 224 species of birds, but what was the point of assembling such a collection if no one could see it? She decided it was time to let the public view her work. She created a display for a show sponsored by the Colorado Agricultural Society.

"The largest collection of Colorado birds we have ever seen is now on exhibition at the Fair Grounds," reported the *Rocky Mountain News.* "They were picked up by Mrs. Maxwell, of Boulder, within six months, count over one hundred different kinds, and are arranged on two large shrubs of cottonwood with a great deal of taste." The paper added that the exhibit was "probably the greatest attraction in the room."

As Martha's reputation grew, she caught the attention of the Smithsonian Institution, one of the world's preeminent natural history research facilities. The institution asked her to provide them with animal specimens, and she offered some that scientists there had never seen before. In return they offered her valuable tips on taxidermy and natural history.

She also befriended Robert Ridgway, one of the world's leading ornithologists. So taken was Ridgway with Martha Maxwell's work that he gave the Rocky Mountain screech owl, which Martha had first identified, the Latin name of *Scops asio maxwelliae*. The honor, he said, was "a deserved tribute to her high attainments in the study of natural history."

In 1874 Martha decided to open a museum in Boulder so that more people would be able to see her work. She crammed into it "every beast of the forest and plains, every bird of the air," the *Boulder News* reported. The mounted animals were arranged in natural settings. Birds perched on branches, a mountain lion lunged from a tree, and a mountain sheep scrambled up a rocky cliff.

Martha's aim was to educate, but she believed that entertainment was an important part of the learning process. She assembled what author Helen Hunt Jackson called "comic groups" of animals, including one scene in which two monkeys played poker. One monkey scowled at the bad hand he'd been dealt, while the other smirked over his aces. The two were so absorbed in the game that they didn't notice a third monkey reaching up from under the table to steal the stakes.

Martha also loved to showcase exotic items in her museum: a reindeer hide from Alaska, a small silk shoe from China, or war clubs from New Zealand. The eclectic collection clearly was ahead of its time. As biographer Benson noted:

> *[Martha's] conception of a museum that would be at once scientific, educational, and popular was remarkably sophisticated, particularly considering the time period and the geographical area*

in which she developed it. Her ideas placed her in the vanguard
of museum philosophy in the 1870s, although there is no evidence
that she drew upon or was influenced by what was happening
elsewhere in the country. And even in the East, the movement that
would see the development of large natural history museums and
similar multifaceted institutions was in its infancy.

Yet few Americans had ever heard of Martha's work on the western frontier. Renowned naturalist William Hornaday once claimed that he created the first habitat display for large mammals in 1879. Whether he knew it or not, Martha had beaten him to it at her museum in Boulder.

Visitors to Martha's museum were enthralled, but there were too few of them to make it a paying proposition. Martha decided to move the museum to the booming city of Denver. But first she wanted to take advantage of an even better opportunity: the Centennial Exposition in Philadelphia. The show was intended to celebrate the nation's one hundredth birthday in grand fashion, with displays of art and the latest technology. Ten million visitors were expected to attend.

Martha was assigned an entire wall in the Kansas-Colorado Building, where she constructed an idyllic mountain scene and populated it with high-country denizens. Another part of the display featured a simulated prairie inhabited by grassland animals. Nearby, she displayed live animals such as prairie dogs and rattlesnakes.

Her sister, Mary Dartt, described the exhibit this way:

Down the rugged descent leaped a little stream of sparkling
water, which expanded at its base into a tiny lake, edged with
pebbles and fringed, as was the brook-side, with growing grass
and fern. The water and the banks which confined it were peo-
pled by aquatic creatures: fish swimming in the lake, turtles

sunning themselves on its half-submerged rocks, while beavers, muskrats, and water-fowl seemed at home upon the margin. Between the cascade and lakelet appeared the irregular vine-fringed mouth of a cave, its dark moss-grown recesses soon lost from sight in the shadowy gloom. Above it upon the upper heights of the mountain side . . . were grouped those animals that frequent the Rocky Mountains: fierce bears, shy mountain sheep, savage mountain lions or pumas, and a multitude of smaller creatures, each in an attitude of lifelike action. On the limited space allowed to represent the plains that stretch eastward from that elevated chain were huge buffaloes, elk, antelope, and their native neighbors.

Visitors marveled over the realism of Martha's mounted animals and were surprised to discover that a woman had not only crafted them but had shot many of the animals herself. Newspaper reporters dubbed Martha the "Colorado huntress." Critics complained that she had wantonly destroyed too many animals. But Martha, a strict vegetarian, tartly replied, "There isn't a day you don't tacitly consent to have some creature killed so that you may eat it. I leave it to you. Which is more cruel? To kill to eat or to kill to immortalize?"

Compliments for Martha's display far outnumbered the criticisms. Some writers even suggested that she was a new model of womanhood— a woman who could maintain her femininity while espousing feminist goals and doing men's work. Martha happily perpetuated this image of herself. Asked about her hunting skills, she told one reporter, "A great many of my birds I have procured myself with a gun—and I am not a masculine woman either. My height is a little less than five feet and I weigh 120 lbs."

Now in her mid-forties, Martha hoped to capitalize on the buzz over her exposition show by arranging more exhibits in Washington, DC, and Philadelphia. She also began work on a book about her life called *On the Plains, and Among the Peaks; or, How Mrs. Maxwell Made Her Natural History Collection.* In this she was assisted by her sister, Mary Dartt, who wrote the final draft. Martha had every reason to be optimistic; she expected her biography and her taxidermy to bring her financial security.

The book was favorably reviewed, but it didn't sell well. And prospects for more shows never materialized. Martha was unsure what to do. James wanted her to return to Colorado, but this idea held little appeal. Instead, she enrolled at the Massachusetts Institute of Technology, where she could study natural history and hobnob with Boston-area feminists and reformers. She loved college life but could not afford the tuition. She was so strapped for cash in 1876 that she took jobs dressing Christmas dolls and managing a restaurant. Three years later, she managed a brief visit to Colorado to see her ailing mother, who had been living in Boulder since the early 1870s. Martha apparently spent little, if any, time visiting her husband during the trip.

When Martha returned to New York, as lonely and penniless as ever, she conceived of yet another moneymaking scheme. She would build a museum and goodie shop at a seaside resort on Long Island. Boosters were predicting a wonderful future for the resort, but many of the expected attractions failed to materialize. Martha's first season in 1880 was disappointing. She had dreamed of making enough money to provide a good home for her daughter, who had finished college at Wellesley in 1878 and had gone back to Colorado to live with her grandparents, the Dartts. Martha was wracked with guilt, knowing she had neglected her daughter for too many years. For her part, Mabel had openly expressed her resentment of her mother's single-minded pursuit of a career.

Mabel once wrote that she thought her mother considered her "an ugly duckling hatched by a thoroughbred hen."

"What did I want?" she continued. "A home, I told her. All my life I had longed for a home and I had never had one. The feminist in mother protested fiercely. What about a career? Making a home, I retorted, seemed to me the finest and most useful career a woman could have."

Mabel took a teaching job in Colorado, while Martha remained in New York, still hoping her luck would turn. But her prospects for success instead grew dimmer, and she became more depressed, ill, and lonely.

"Never see any one to speak with—imagine myself shipwrecked but you know I care but little for the society of any except my dear ones who are far away," she wrote to Mabel in 1880.

Soon, Martha learned that she was dying of ovarian cancer, and Mabel rushed to New York to be with her at the end.

"Mother was so pitifully glad to see me that it almost broke my heart," Mabel later wrote in her memoir, *Thanks to Abigail.*

Martha died in her daughter's arms on May 31, 1881, just two months shy of her fiftieth birthday. Despite Mabel's disappointment in her mother's choices, she resolved to save Martha's natural history collection, which was now big enough to fill a two-story barn. But she could not find a buyer, and she had to move it into storage. Mabel returned to Colorado, where she married a Boulder doctor, Charles Brace.

Eventually an entrepreneur purchased Martha's collection and put it on display in Saratoga Springs, New York. He charged visitors twenty-five cents to see it. When business ebbed, he stored the collection heedlessly in a musty barn. Years later, university representatives from Yale and Colorado examined it in hopes of adding it to their collections, but they determined that it was too moth-eaten to be of any value.

Martha's work had once represented the pinnacle of taxidermy and natural history. Now, tattered and decayed, it symbolized the sad turn her life had taken.

Toward the end of her life she wrote:

I am condemned for having an ambition to be something more than the common lot of mortals. Well I have a desire to live for something more than the gratification of those who cannot appreciate the sacrifice. Yes I would do something which shall follow me, doing good to others after I am gone.

Caroline Nichols Churchill

(1833–1926)

WIELDER OF PISTOL AND PEN

Caroline Nichols Churchill was jolted from a sound sleep by a hammering on the door of her Georgetown, Colorado, boarding room.

"I paid for that room!" a man bellowed from the hallway. "You've got to get out of it."

It was two in the morning, and Caroline was exhausted after a long day selling newspaper subscriptions in the mining communities west of Boulder. But she quickly shook the grogginess from her head.

"You leave that door instantly or you will have a ball put into your carcass, if not more than one," she called back.

"Fire away," sneered the intruder.

Not one to be intimidated, Caroline snatched up her pistol, aimed, and pulled the trigger three times in quick succession. Three slugs tore through the door, but Caroline heard no cries of pain or thud of a body against the floorboards. She figured the man had ducked out of harm's way and slunk quietly downstairs. She waited until morning to complain to the desk clerk about the intrusion, but instead of offering his sympathy, he demanded that she pay for the night's lodging, however restless it might have been.

True to her nature, Caroline made sure she had the last word about the incident. When she got back to her Denver home that summer of 1879, she described the affair in her feisty feminist newspaper, *The Antelope*. Six weeks later, she learned that the inn had closed because business had plummeted.

"Such is the fate of tyrants," she gloated.

As the innkeeper discovered, Caroline was not one to hold her fire—with her pistol or her pen. Most often her targets were men, the majority

CAROLINE NICHOLS CHURCHILL
At Forty Years.

Caroline Nichols Churchill History Colorado, Biographical Portrait File

of whom she considered to be "animals" responsible for "all the evils of society." But she also pointed her poison pen at liquor, tobacco, dance halls, the Catholic Church, inefficient garbage collectors, and Denver mining magnate Horace Tabor, who had abandoned his wife for a younger and prettier woman.

What did Caroline campaign *for?* Equal rights for women was at the top of her list. Her editorials championed vocational education for girls, pensions for mothers with dependent children, and, of course, a woman's right to vote. She crusaded for suffrage for years, paving the way for the 1893 vote that extended the franchise to Colorado women. Caroline heralded the event with a typically enthusiastic headline: "Western Women Wild With Joy!" It was the highlight of a writing career that spanned more than three decades in Colorado.

Caroline was born in Ontario, Canada, to American-born parents on December 23, 1833. At the age of thirteen, she was sent to live with her maternal grandmother in the United States, where she briefly attended school. She considered herself a "natural reader and a good speller for her years and opportunities." At fourteen, she returned home and put her education to good use. She spent three months teaching private school, using her mother's sitting room for a classroom. For her efforts she earned a total of twenty-five dollars.

In her 1909 autobiography, *Active Footsteps,* Caroline provided a perceptive description of herself:

> *Great animation in countenance when talking. Her chief attraction. Constitution rather light; health seldom perfect. A student by mental temperament. Not mathematical nor mechanical, but an abstract reasoner. Order of brain, statesmanship, philosophical and poetical. Not really great in anything but perseverance, firmness, and self-respect. Longs for a more ideal civilization. . . . In childhood seldom took risks that children do, in climbing, jumping*

from high places, and so forth. Was called lazy, and an inveter-
ate old granny, for the above reasons. Was quiet and retiring,
preferring books and music to society. . . . Had a remarkable
musical voice, for strength and sweetness. A memory that few
could equal in the way of events of general importance and
statistics, but could not remember the component parts of sour
milk griddle cakes.

In her early twenties, Caroline bowed to convention and married, since, as she put it years later, "people did not know what else to do with girls, as there were few avenues of employment for them." The union was apparently an unhappy one. She barely mentioned her husband in her autobiography, other than to say that he died in the early 1860s, leaving her with a young daughter to raise. An unsatisfying marriage may well have contributed to her harsh views on men, but Caroline also seemed oddly detached from her daughter, whom she also mentioned only briefly in her memoir. The girl was adopted and raised by one of Caroline's sisters.

In 1857 Caroline took a teaching job in Minnesota, where she befriended a newspaper editor who was an ardent feminist and abolitionist. This friendship reinforced her own political views—and introduced her to the business of journalism. In 1870 she moved to California, hoping the climate would relieve the coughing fits that had plagued her much of her life. She wrote poetry and books and then, while visiting Colorado in 1879 on a book tour, discovered that the high altitude and low humidity she found there were invigorating. This, she decided, was the ideal place to realize her long-standing dream of publishing her own newspaper.

Not only was the climate better, but Coloradans were receptive to her reformist views. Living on the frontier, they were open to new ideas and less tied to tradition.

"All reforms take root in new countries sooner than in older communities," Caroline observed.

At the age of forty-seven, she set up shop in Denver, a bustling city of about thirty thousand people. The first issue of her monthly paper, *The Antelope*, rolled off the press in June 1879. Caroline stood on a street corner and peddled a thousand copies for a dime apiece. The papers were gone by noon. Three years later she decided to publish weekly instead of monthly. She also renamed her newspaper *The Queen Bee*—an epithet that some people began to apply to Caroline herself. Working from home, she kept as busy as a hive of bees, writing, editing, and selling ads and subscriptions. She did hire others to print the paper but often complained about how unreliable they were.

In the late 1800s Caroline was one of an estimated two thousand women working as journalists in the Far West. But only a handful of them, like Caroline, published and edited their own papers.

"On a national level, she ran the country's first all-woman newsroom," according to Colorado historian Jeanne Varnell, "published one of the first, if not the first, women's emancipation newspapers, and was a leading feminist of her time."

Caroline traveled extensively through five western states to sell ads and subscriptions and gather news. On one such trip she was startled and offended when her wagon driver propositioned her. When she shunned his advances, he steered the wagon off a low bridge and jumped off in time to save himself. Caroline was thrown from the wagon, knocked unconscious, and badly bruised—but once again she got even. She exposed the driver's skulduggery in her paper's next edition. He was fired, and a few months later he committed suicide. Caroline reported that his neighbors greeted his death with a "sense of relief."

On another trip Caroline roomed at an apartment house in southern New Mexico, where several men tried to goad her into partying with them. She responded by dumping a bucket of water on the chief instigator. She learned the next day that the man was planning his revenge, so she hiked out of town, carrying her forty-pound bag on her back.

"If women could have a hand in executing the laws for their own, these shameful performances would become of rarer occurrence," she later wrote.

Caroline often argued in her paper that women could solve many of society's problems if only given the chance. After all, she said, women had saved countless lives by spearheading the temperance movement.

"If woman continues in mental development, there will be found a remedy for most of the serious social ills that exist," she said. "We are living out the adage all have heard reiterated so many times, that two heads are better than one if one is a woman's. . . . Men do not know all there is to be known and put into execution for the welfare of the race."

To this end Caroline kept up a steady drumbeat for suffrage. If women were equal partners with men, she argued, they could help solve Colorado's economic woes. But she conceded that women had to take more responsibility and be more assertive in order to earn equality. She once wrote:

> We are aware of the jealousies of many husbands in regard to any public work which the wife may be interested in. But women should remember that all the evils of society are caused by the bad management of men, and women are greatly to blame for folding their hands and permitting this state of things.

Caroline also fretted that too many women wasted time on trivial matters. She complained of being stopped on the street by women who only wanted to engage in small talk. Women, she said, "seem to have very little idea of the importance of business time."

Caroline had other prejudices—and she didn't try to hide them. She thought Southerners displayed a "coarse familiarity" that was "repugnant to the Northern-bred person." And she once attacked Arab men by claiming they found wives by clubbing women and dragging them into their tents.

Caroline aimed her sharpest barbs at American men, particularly those opposed to suffrage. She once asserted that the antisuffrage editor of the *Solid Muldoon* in Ouray was going bald "because his brain could not furnish sufficient vitality or nerve . . . to sustain the growth of hair."

Not surprisingly, Caroline's tirades spawned enemies. She was blackballed by members of the Colorado Editor's Press Association, though she claimed the snub didn't bother her. She said she had no desire to mix with a "class of men so much below par with the women of the country."

Still, some men were attracted to Caroline, a comely woman with high cheekbones, dainty nose, fair skin, and full lips. She always rebuffed their advances. By her mid-forties, she declared that she was "fool proof as well as man proof." All she needed, she once told a friend, was a strong will and some good books, a pen and paper, and a few pets to keep her company.

By 1882, when Caroline began publishing on a weekly basis, her circulation had reached 2,500—the highest circulation, she claimed, for any weekly between San Francisco and Kansas City. But the good times wouldn't last. The nationwide Silver Panic of 1893 clobbered Colorado's economy, and Caroline's paper wasn't spared. She had published without missing an issue for more than a decade but was finally forced to quit. She announced that she was closing for "repairs and different arrangements due to use of machinery in printing and general cheapening of literature."

Caroline moved to Colorado Springs to live with one of her sisters. She continued to put out her paper intermittently, and before she died in 1926 at the age of ninety-two, she wrote *Active Footsteps,* a fascinating book filled with an odd assortment of anecdotes and eccentric opinions.

Caroline chose to write the book in third person, referring to herself as Mrs. Churchill. She used this device, she said, so that "as much as possible, the ego might be hidden." Yet she portrayed herself as a strong-willed woman, very sure of her place in the world, a woman who did "wonderful work under most difficult circumstances." Although she conceded that famous feminists Susan B. Anthony and Lucy Stone had many noble accomplishments, she pointedly noted that they had never achieved the "political emancipation" of a single state, as she had in Colorado. Unabashedly, she added, "It is not at all likely that another woman on the continent could under the same conditions accomplish as much."

Elizabeth "Baby" Doe Tabor

(1854–1935)

SILVER QUEEN

The Willard Hotel in Washington, DC, had been transformed into a "fairyland of flowers" for the 1883 wedding of US Senator Horace Tabor and Elizabeth "Baby" Doe. The centerpiece of the event was a massive wedding bell made of white roses, topped by a floral cupid's bow and an arrow tipped with violets. A canopy of flowers obscured the ceiling. It was a ceremony fit for royalty, but Horace could easily afford it. His Colorado mines had made him one of the wealthiest men in the country.

The wedding was one of the most stunning the nation's capital had ever seen, and the bride was by far the most dazzling sight of the evening. Baby paraded down the aisle in a $7,500 white satin gown and a $75,000 diamond necklace.

"I have never seen a more beautiful bride," gushed one guest, President Chester A. Arthur.

The *Washington Post* agreed, proclaiming the new Mrs. Tabor to be a "veritable beauty—blonde, with face and form alike almost ideal in their lovely proportions. She is medium height and well rounded in figure and of charming manner, with vivacious and entertaining conversational power."

Another newspaper said Baby had a "face that would be called beautiful among beauties."

In the face of such flattery, Baby no doubt assumed that her marriage marked the beginning of a life of wealth and leisure, a life she had coveted since childhood. Her new husband was delighted, too. At the age of fifty-two, he had married a striking woman twenty-four

Baby Doe Tabor Denver Public Library, Western History Collection, X-21980

years his junior, and he had only recently become a player on the national political scene.

But beyond the silver lining, storm clouds were amassing. The wedding had drawn dozens of senators and representatives, cabinet heads, and captains of industry, but the wives of the dignitaries had stayed away in protest. To their Victorian sensibilities, the fact that Baby had been Tabor's mistress was disgraceful and unforgivable. Likewise, the Catholic priest who married the Tabors erupted in rage after he learned that he'd been tricked into marrying two divorcees. He refused to sign the marriage certificate. He relented only when ordered to do so by his superiors, who apparently had been persuaded to intervene by Horace's gifts of money.

The atmosphere grew even chillier when the press reported that Horace and Baby had actually been married secretly in St. Louis three months before Horace's divorce from his first wife, Augusta. If the rumor was true, Horace was a bigamist in the eyes of the law. The newlyweds lamely argued that their St. Louis ceremony was just a sentimental gesture and not a legal marriage. Their argument was unconvincing, but the criticism finally blew over.

This would not be the last controversy to swirl around Baby Doe Tabor. For most of her adult life, society would shun her because of her passionate loyalty to an already married man. She would never win the acceptance she craved, but her story would captivate the public as she rose from rags to riches and sank into rags once again. Her history inspired a movie, an opera, a number of books, and many news stories.

Baby's remarkable life began unremarkably. She was born September 25, 1854, in Oshkosh, Wisconsin, the fifth of fourteen children of middle-class parents, Peter and Elizabeth Nellis McCourt. The couple named her Elizabeth, or Lizzie for short. Her brother James called her Baby, and the nickname stuck.

As a teen she became known as the "Belle of Oshkosh." With her curly hair, blue eyes, creamy complexion, and full figure, she caught the eye of many men. One of her admirers was Harvey Doe, a handsome charmer who loved to sing and play piano. Baby thought Harvey would be a good catch; after all, his family had amassed a fortune from investments in timber and mining.

Baby had long dreamed of marrying into money, so she wed Harvey in 1877. She was twenty-two; he was twenty-three. As a wedding gift, the Doe family presented them with the title to a silver mine near Central City, Colorado. No doubt it seemed to Baby like the opportunity of a lifetime, but when the couple moved to Colorado, Baby discovered that her new husband had no knack for mining—or much of anything else, for that matter. Occasionally, he'd scrounge up enough money to hire work crews for a few days, but then the money would dry up, his interest would wane, and the mine would shut down again. Harvey drifted from one job to another.

Exasperated, Baby took matters into her own hands. Donning miner's togs, she began hacking at the rocks with a pick and running a mule team to haul timbers. Neighbors were horrified to see a woman dressed like a man doing such difficult work, but Baby shrugged off their insulting remarks. She was determined to make a go of the mine.

By the summer of 1878, Baby rarely saw Harvey. He disappeared for days at a time, never explaining where he went or what he did. Harvey was gone when, by some accounts, impoverished and lonely Baby gave birth to their stillborn son. One of the few friends helping her through that difficult time was Jake Sands, a handsome New Yorker who ran a clothing store. How close the two were is still open to debate. Baby wrote in her diary of sitting on the schoolhouse steps with Jacob: "He kissed me three times and oh! how he loved me and he does now."

Baby decided she wanted a divorce. She tracked down her increasingly erratic husband in Denver, but he refused to acquiesce. So she followed him secretly until she spied him entering a brothel. This gave her the evidence she needed, and a judge granted her the divorce on March 19, 1880.

Jake Sands convinced Baby to move with him to Leadville, which was booming with mining activity in the mountains west of Denver. Fortune seekers had pushed Leadville's population to fifteen thousand—making it Colorado's second-largest city after Denver—and Baby figured she could improve her fortunes there, too.

Three years earlier, Horace Austin Warner Tabor had come to Leadville with his wife, Augusta, and their son, Maxcy, to open a miners' supply store and post office. For the previous eighteen years, they had run a series of struggling stores in the Colorado mining camps. Horace, a swarthy and muscular New Englander, had extended credit for years to customers who were short on money but long on optimism. This practice had not paid off—not, at least, until 1878. That's when prospectors George Hook and August Rische talked Horace into grubstaking their claim on nearby Fryer Hill. Much to everyone's surprise, Hook and Rische discovered a high-grade vein of silver, and Horace was entitled to a third of the profits. His $64.75 investment yielded thousands of dollars within weeks. Horace shrewdly reinvested his profits in other mining properties. By late 1879 these mines were producing more than a million dollars' worth of ore each year.

Besides buying more mines, Horace built an opera house and invested in a gas company, newspaper, telephone companies, and the First National Bank of Denver. He also sought political power. He served as Leadville's first mayor, and in 1878 he was elected lieutenant governor of Colorado. In a few short years, he had rocketed from obscurity to political prominence and princely wealth. He was Colorado's bonanza king.

But Augusta, his stiff and stern wife, was less impressed with her husband's accomplishments. She badgered him to spend less money on entertainment and risky investments and to curb his other excesses. Horace responded by avoiding Augusta as much as possible. He had purchased a twenty-room house in Denver, and he left her there while he spent much of his time tending to business in Leadville, where he had an apartment and office. He also had a chance to enjoy Leadville's tempting nightlife.

One evening on his way to dinner, he was introduced to a striking young lady with blonde ringlets and an eye-catching figure. He invited her to join him at his table, and Baby was delighted to accept. She had heard all about the wealthy businessman. They talked all night and ended up infatuated with each other, despite their differences in age. Baby was twenty-five and Horace was forty-nine. Soon, Baby had accepted the millionaire's offer to pay her debts and move her into a luxury suite at the Clarendon Hotel.

Occasionally, Horace and Baby would venture out in public together, but she would pull a veil down over her face because Horace was still married. Local wags dubbed her the "hussy in the veil." She resented the talk and longed for a conventional marriage, but Horace was reluctant to seek a divorce from Augusta. That might seriously damage his ballooning political ambitions, he thought.

Horace failed to recognize yet another threat to his aspirations: the growing gap between himself and his workers. He refused to bow to his miners' demands for an eight-hour day and better pay. When the workers went on strike, Horace brought in the militia to force them to back down. The strikers became so desperate that they finally returned to work without winning a single concession. Horace won the skirmish but paid a heavy price by creating many enemies who never forgot his heavy-handed tactics.

Horace grew more and more alienated from Augusta. She called him a fool for exploiting his workers and wasting money. She also annoyed him by purchasing a one-third interest in Denver's Windsor Hotel, where he had rented a suite for Baby. This allowed Augusta, as an owner, to plant herself in the lobby, where she could do her needlework and keep an eye open for her wandering husband and his paramour. She hoped her vigil would shame Horace and Baby into separating.

Her efforts only drove Horace farther away. He once told Baby, "You're always so gay and laughing, and yet you're so brave. Augusta is a damned brave woman, too, but she's powerful disagreeable about it."

Horace wanted a divorce, but he had to handle the situation with care. Divorces were uncommon and unaccepted at the time, and they could imperil a political career. He sent an emissary to Augusta to request a divorce, and she countered by filing for a property settlement, a legal move meant to protect her interest in the family fortune. Secretly, Horace filed for divorce miles away in Durango, where he owned a mine and could use his clout. An unscrupulous judge signed the court order in March 1882, although Augusta later insisted she was never served with a summons. A few months later, Horace and Baby took separate trains to St. Louis, where they married in a secret ceremony on September 30.

In early 1883 Augusta finally agreed to an official divorce but told the presiding judge in Denver, "Not willingly, oh God, not willingly." The judge awarded her $250,000 and some property, including her twenty-room house. Colorado's newspapers delighted in printing all the dirty details, including Augusta's observation that Horace had "changed a great deal" as he used to "detest" women like Baby. Augusta predicted Baby would abandon Horace if his finances flagged.

"She wants his money and will hang on to him as long as he has got a nickel," she said. "She don't want an old man."

Augusta was wrong. She had misjudged Baby's devotion to Horace. Baby was delighted to be the new Mrs. Tabor; she was finally free to drop the veil and be seen with her husband in public. Horace regained his confidence, too, as mining enterprises, including a new one called the Matchless, generated healthy profits. Even his political prospects looked promising.

Horace was angling for an appointment to the US Senate after incumbent Colorado Senator Henry Teller was appointed to President Arthur's cabinet. Horace reportedly spent $200,000 on the campaign for Teller's old job but met with resistance from Coloradans who remembered how he had mistreated his mine workers and scandalized the state with his private life. Journalists called him an "utter disgrace" and a "shambling, illiterate boor."

"He is a social and political outcast in all senses of the word," a Denver paper reported.

In the late nineteenth century, US senators were not elected, but were appointed by a state's legislature. Colorado's lawmakers rebuffed Horace's desire to go to Washington as Teller's permanent replacement. But in recognition of his support for the Republican Party, they offered him a consolation prize: He could fill out the last thirty days of Teller's term until a new senator took office.

Horace swallowed his pride and accepted. At least he would have a few weeks in the national spotlight. And his time in the Senate would allow him to give Baby one of the most ornate wedding ceremonies the nation's capital had ever seen.

Horace's political aspirations did not end with his short stint in the Senate. There was talk he might run for president, though he never did. He sought the GOP nomination for governor in 1884 and 1888, but he was unsuccessful both times. He worked hard to build the Republican Party, but it never united behind him.

Horace also continued to invest around the globe in industries as diverse as mining, banking, agriculture, manufacturing, shipping, logging, newspapers, and insurance. Some newspapers estimated that his empire was worth as much as $10 million, although Augusta put the figure at $9 million in court documents. His son, Maxcy, guessed, probably more accurately, that Horace's business empire was worth between $5 million and $7.5 million at its peak. Whatever the true figure, there was no disputing that Horace Tabor was one of Colorado's wealthiest men.

The crown jewels of his empire were his opera houses in Leadville and Denver. The Tabor Opera House, which opened in 1879 at a cost of

$60,000, was Leadville's most elegant building. It once hosted a lecture by Oscar Wilde. In 1881 the curtain opened on the Tabor Grand Opera House in Denver. The $800,000, five-story brick building rivaled the world's grandest opera houses and was festooned with Belgian carpets, French tapestries, Japanese cherry wood, Honduran mahogany, French silk, and Italian marble.

Horace and Baby loved the opera house, which drew such internationally acclaimed performers as Sarah Bernhardt and Maurice Barrymore. Sometimes the Tabors entertained friends in their box above the stage, and Baby hoped the theater might help her fulfill her dream of ascending Denver's social ladder. Once, when a newspaper reporter called on Baby, she told him she had been "flooded with invitations from the very best people of Denver to attend all sorts of affairs. I have decided not to accept them so as not to create jealousy among the society leaders of Denver." In truth, Baby was always snubbed by Denver's social leaders, who were still appalled by her sordid involvement in the breakup of Horace and Augusta's marriage.

Horace helped salve Baby's wounded pride by purchasing a pretentious $54,000 mansion and nicely landscaped grounds that covered a city block at Thirteenth Avenue and Sherman Street. The pair outfitted the house with the finest furniture and works of art, including five paintings of Baby. These were displayed where visitors could easily admire them. A staff of five ran the house. A large carriage house out back sheltered three carriages and six horses. Dozens of peacocks strutted around the three-acre grounds. When snooty neighbors complained about the bronze statues of naked Greek gods that dotted their property, Baby sarcastically ordered her servants to drape costumes over them.

Few Denver residents came to visit the Tabors in their mansion, and Baby consoled herself by clipping inspirational newspaper and magazine articles and gluing them into scrapbooks. One article likely boosted her battered self-esteem. Titled "Should Divorced Women Be

Received into Society?" it concluded that the "reasoning that would keep a divorced woman from society would send to prison the merchant who was robbed by his confidential and trusted cashier."

Baby also drew comfort from frequent letters Horace sent her while traveling to inspect his far-flung business ventures.

"My darling, darling wife, you are near me even when I can't see you," he said in one letter typical of the 250 that she saved. "Your love guides me in even the simplest transactions of life."

Motherhood occupied much of Baby's time. Daughter Elizabeth Bonduel Lily was born July 13, 1884, and Rose Mary Echo Silver Dollar was born December 17, 1889. Baby also gave birth to a son, who died just a few hours later.

Long resentful of the fuss made by the Catholic priest who had married her, Baby was delighted when another priest gave her a medallion blessed by the pope in honor of Lily's birth.

"My own cup of bliss was overflowing for some time," she declared, "and I forgot all about the jealous cats and sanctimonious old battle-axes of Denver. I was a mother."

Baby treated Lily like a princess. She fastened her daughter's lavish clothes with gold pins embedded with diamonds. For her christening, Lily wore a lace and velvet gown worth more than $15,000. The "Little Silver Princess" was featured in magazines across the United States and Europe.

Yet even international attention did not open the door to Denver society for Baby. Legend has it that she once exacted revenge by bringing a fussy infant Lily to a Tabor Grand Opera performance. When she carried her wailing daughter into the Tabor box, actor Edwin Booth interrupted his performance and objected to the noise. Horace reportedly got the last word by banning Booth from any further appearances. Most of the opera house performers treated Baby with the deference and attention she craved, and she reciprocated with lavish dinners for them at her mansion.

Baby's wealth did not blind her to the needs of others. When Colorado women fought for the right to vote in 1893, Baby provided them with office space from which to wage their campaign. She also contributed to charities and churches. On Christmas Eve she distributed food, toys, and money in the Denver slums.

By the early 1890s Baby had financial worries of her own. Horace's mines had struggled for years, and matters got worse when the federal government stopped using silver as the nation's monetary standard. Horace's other business ventures stumbled as well. He had plowed too much money into speculative enterprises and spent months in Mexico, hoping his mines there would replenish his fortune. Baby stayed in Denver, raising her daughters, fending off creditors, and managing her husband's business affairs as best she could.

"She must be given a great deal of credit during those crucial years, 1893–1894, when she held the line, separated from her husband much of the time and under increasing creditor pressures," said Duane A. Smith in his biography, *Horace Tabor*. "Tabor placed complete faith in his wife, giving her power of attorney to act on his behalf."

Unfortunately, the Mexican mines never amounted to much, and creditors began seizing the Tabors' properties. In 1896 they lost the Grand Opera House and a block of business buildings. Then creditors seized their home. Some accounts claim that when city workers arrived at the mansion to shut off the lights and water, Baby shouted at them, "Remind your employers of the many contributions Tabor has made to Denver. Never mind, we will revive the Matchless and then everything will be as it should be again."

The Tabors' fall from fortune was precipitous. They had been worth millions; now they were left with just a few personal possessions and a handful of worthless mining claims and stocks. Baby, who became an increasingly devout Catholic in the 1890s, sent the mother superior of the St. Clara Orphans' Home a letter dripping with desperation: "We want your prayers & entreaties to God to save our properties and if they are saved we will build the new wing on your home and pay the debt that is now on it and do as much as possible for your home every month."

Some Denver residents assumed that Baby, still attractive in her thirties, would dump her paunchy, balding, and impoverished husband for a younger man with better prospects. She did have suitors, including a few of Horace's longtime associates, but she rebuffed those men who discreetly approached her.

"What kind of wife do you think I am?" she angrily told one admirer.

Baby stubbornly believed in Horace and his ability to make a comeback. Now in his sixties, he roamed the mountain mining camps, hoping to discover another claim that would reverse his family's downward spiral. But his old luck eluded him when he launched mining operations west of Boulder in Cripple Creek and Ward. To make matters worse, he was earning just three dollars a day, and his frail body suffered from the rigors of mining work.

In 1898 life began to look brighter. Horace was appointed postmaster of Denver at what was then a healthy salary of $3,500 a year. He was able to rent a comfortable suite at the Windsor Hotel for his family.

A few months later, Baby took her children to New York City, hoping that a change in climate would cure Lily of a respiratory illness. Horace missed his family and fretted over Baby's shortage of money and her own health. She had developed neuralgia, acute pain that follows the course of a nerve.

"I am very homesick for you Babe and for the joyous children," he wrote his wife.

In April, shortly after Baby and the girls returned to Denver, Horace started suffering from stomach problems. He took to his bed and Baby summoned doctors, who diagnosed a ruptured appendix. The doctors agreed there wasn't much they could do; Horace, at sixty-eight, was too old to survive an operation. The day before he died, Horace was baptized into the Catholic faith.

"This is the happiest moment of my life," he told his wife. "I am at peace and resigned to the will of God."

Early accounts of Tabor's life claimed that he told Baby on his deathbed never to sell the Matchless Mine because it would someday make millions. The myth enhanced her image as a loyal widow, since she lived her last thirty years in a ramshackle cabin next to the mine.

By the time Horace died in the spring of 1899, most Coloradans had forgotten any animosity they had once held for him. State officials allowed his body to lie in state at the Capitol, and thousands of well-wishers streamed past to pay their respects. Baby was comforted to know that her husband had finally won the "prestige due a great man."

With Horace's death Baby had to face a harsh reality: She and her daughters were destitute once again. Horace had left them little besides the Matchless Mine in Leadville, and creditors were angling to seize that.

Perhaps Baby could have led a comfortable life if she had moved back to Wisconsin to live with her family. But she decided to stay in Colorado to be close to Horace's spirit. She moved into a tenement building and began prowling Denver's financial district, hoping to badger old acquaintances for a grubstake to reopen the Matchless. One sympathetic millionaire friend wrote her a check, and Baby and her daughters lived off the money for almost a decade.

Baby eventually returned to Leadville with hopes of reopening the Matchless Mine. Lily loathed the idea of mining and was embarrassed to learn from Leadville friends of her mother's sordid past. When a relative invited Lily to come to Chicago, she jumped at the chance to escape from painful memories.

"Nobody but a fool still believes the mine will ever produce again," she lectured her mother before leaving.

Lily never returned to Colorado. She eventually moved to Milwaukee, Wisconsin, where she married a cousin, John Last, and raised three children.

Baby's younger daughter, who went by the name of Silver Dollar, was a coin of a different color. Like Baby, she was adventurous, attractive, and willing to use her femininity to get what she wanted. She also was a romantic who loved to flirt and write poetry. Before long she was partying with Leadville's married livery owner.

Well aware of the dangers of such a relationship, Baby persuaded her daughter to move to Denver, where she landed a job with the *Denver Times*. But the job lasted little longer than the time it takes ink to dry on paper. Silver Dollar then wrote a melodramatic novel, *Star of Blood*, but it sold only a few hundred copies. Next, she founded a weekly literary journal, but it too flopped. She tried but failed to work as a movie actress, a waitress, and a belly dancer, and she had no better luck in her quest for love. She got pregnant, her lover disappeared, and she suffered a miscarriage.

Despondent, Silver Dollar left for Chicago, telling Baby that she planned to enter a convent. To devout Baby, this was wonderful news. From then on, when people asked about Silver Dollar, Baby always insisted that her daughter was in a nunnery.

The truth, however, was otherwise. Silver Dollar became addicted to drugs and drink and careened from one lover to another. She could not hold a job, even as a strip dancer, because she staggered too much to stay on the stage.

Silver Dollar's tragic life ended in 1925, when she was only thirty-six. While living in a flophouse, she was badly burned by a kettle of boiling water. The police found her in bed, naked, drunk, and barely alive. She claimed she had accidentally spilled the water off the stove. Police suspected that an ill-tempered former lover was to blame. They took the man into custody but released him when a coroner's jury couldn't determine whether she had been murdered or killed accidentally.

When reporters pressed Baby for answers, she voiced her skepticism that the dead woman was her daughter. "All a pack of lies," Baby said. "That woman isn't my Silver. She is in a convent near Chicago."

Baby faced yet another crisis when creditors foreclosed on the Matchless Mine. Over the years, she had worked the mine herself and even persuaded others to work there. They soon abandoned their efforts after realizing that the flooded mine shafts could never produce anything of value. New owners of the mine did allow Baby to continue living in a cabin at the mine site.

Baby kept food on the table by accepting "loans" from friends and by making do with very little. Instead of buying shoes, she wrapped her feet in burlap and tied it on with twine. She stuffed newspaper under her clothes to keep warm. When she caught colds, she doctored herself with doses of turpentine and lard. She picked up brisket and loaves of stale bread at a store below Fryer Hill. "Put those on my tab," she would say. Eventually, a town charity fund would pay the bill.

Now alone and in her seventies, Baby became more eccentric, reclusive, and religious. During her lonely months on the mountain, she immersed herself in mysticism. She believed that she could communicate with the dead. In moments of clarity she would admit to friends that the Matchless would never produce again, but she never wavered in her loyalty to her husband's memory.

"Her lonely 35-year vigil was a dedication to the man she loved and expiation for past sins," said Caroline Bancroft, who wrote a biography of Baby. "The Matchless was an altar where, with her life as a lighted candle, she held perpetual service—and upon which she finally sacrificed herself."

As people heard of Baby's loyalty, she became a celebrity of sorts once again. Tourists traveled up the winding road to [the] mine in order to see her. Sometimes she would emerge from her shack to sign autographs and pose for pictures.

Baby was last seen trudging to town to pick up groceries on February 20, 1935. She caught a ride home in a delivery truck as a winter storm swooped down from the mountain. The storm lingered for days, and neighbors saw smoke coming from Baby's chimney until another blizzard obliterated the view. When the skies cleared on March 7, the smoke had disappeared. Friends broke through six-foot-tall drifts and found Baby's frozen body on the floor. Among her modest possessions were only two wrinkled dollar bills and a handful of coins.

After quiet funerals in Leadville and Denver, eighty-one-year-old Baby was buried next to Horace at Calvary Cemetery in Denver. The only relatives to pay their last respects were her brothers, Willard and Philip McCourt. Her daughter Lily refused to come from Wisconsin and even denied to reporters that she was Baby's daughter.

Although Baby's life ended pitifully, her story didn't die with her. It has been featured in books, magazine articles, and a 1932 movie, *Silver Dollar.* Her legend also inspired *The Ballad of Baby Doe,* one of the most frequently performed operas in the nation since its debut in 1956. More recently, her fans, who call themselves "Doe Heads," created a website, BabyDoe.org, devoted to articles, photographs, and all else related to their historical heroine.

Baby's spirit has remained alive, too, on the mountainside above Leadville. The mine site has been restored and opened as the Matchless Mine–Baby Doe Tabor Museum. Visitors can peer into the mine, examine the heavy-duty equipment used to recover the ore, and inspect Baby's meager personal belongings. They might even sense the presence of the guardian of the Matchless Mine, one of the most loyal women the West has ever known.

As John Burke says in his book *The Legend of Baby Doe,* Baby's "ramshackle quarters outside Leadville have become a sort of shrine to the spirit of the mythic West. [It is] easy enough to imagine . . . that something is astir."

POLLY PRY

(1857–1938)

PUGNACIOUS JOURNALIST

Harry Tammen and Frederick Bonfils, owners of the *Denver Post*, were arguing with W. W. Anderson in their newsroom on a winter day in 1900. Furiously, they accused the lawyer of taking unfair advantage of a man their newspaper was trying to help.

"You're a cheapskate and a liar!" Tammen shouted, prompting Anderson to leap to his feet and raise a fist. But Bonfils swung first, opening a wound under the lawyer's left eye. Polly Pry, one of the paper's most colorful and renowned reporters, pleaded with the men to stop fighting. Anderson snatched his hat and scurried toward the door, with Bonfils and Tammen in close pursuit.

Anderson slammed the door as he left, but it popped back open, and two gunshots rang out. Bonfils slumped to the floor. Anderson rushed back into the room, a smoking pistol in his hand, and marched toward Tammen, who raised his left arm to ward off the coming salvo. Anderson fired two more shots, which smashed into Tammen's arm.

Polly, who had earned a national reputation for her fearless pursuit of the news, rushed between Tammen and Anderson and ordered the lawyer to put down his gun. Anderson ignored her plea and tried to reach around her to squeeze off another shot. He finally gave up as she persistently blocked his way and shouted at him to leave.

"I'll call the police," he said as he backed away.

"Not the police, a doctor; you have done murder enough," Polly retorted.

Anderson whirled toward the door and stalked out of the *Post* building. Police arrested him a short time later, but he did not seem remorseful.

Polly Pry History Colorado, Biographical Portrait File

He figured he had done Denver a big favor. After all, the irascible Post owners had created legions of enemies with their editorial attacks.

As it turned out, jurors couldn't bring themselves to convict Anderson, despite the strong evidence against him. His trial resulted in a hung jury, and Anderson went free. Tammen and Bonfils recovered from their wounds, and Polly went on to experience many more adrenaline-filled adventures. For three decades she reported on wars, violent labor strikes, mining disasters, bizarre murder cases, and other sensational events, earning a reputation as one of the country's most colorful and courageous journalists.

"Her work was always militant," according to Ishbel Ross, author of *Ladies of the Press*. "She scorned the conventional sob story and could out-match most of her masculine competitors in getting what she was after."

Along the way Polly had to overcome the resentment of male colleagues who believed that women belonged in the kitchen, not the newsroom. But as she scored scoop after scoop, many had to admit, as one did, that "for a woman, Polly Pry was pretty damned good."

Polly was born in Kentucky in 1857 to James and Mary Campbell. Her parents named her Leonel Ross Campbell, and the family called her Nell. She took the pen name Polly Pry when she became a journalist.

As a child Polly was sent to study at a girl's school in St. Louis. There she caught the eye of George Anthony, a handsome young man whose family had amassed a fortune building railroads. Small wonder that Anthony was smitten. Polly was blossoming into an outgoing, bright, blonde-haired beauty. Years later, a *Denver Post* reporter would gush that she had a "gift of conversation worthy of the French court," and her beauty was "in the statuesque tradition of a Lillian Russell."

Anthony persuaded Polly to elope, even though she was only fifteen and he was many years older. They moved to Mexico, where Anthony was overseeing construction of the Mexican Central Railroad. They lived in a private railroad car and were occasional guests at the palace of Mexican President Porfirio Diaz.

Polly loved Mexico at first, but after a few years she tired of both the country and her marriage. She left her husband and headed for New York City where, using family connections, she landed a job at the *World* newspaper. At the time it was considered unladylike for a woman to use her real name in a byline, so she adopted the pen name by which she was known for the rest of her life.

Polly soon proved to be adept at ferreting out information, crafting compelling stories, and beating next-to-impossible deadlines. But her job paid only six dollars a week, so she switched to the more lucrative task of writing romance stories for magazines. Cranking out one piece a week, she earned enough to pay her bills and help her struggling parents, who had moved to Denver.

In 1898 she took a train to Colorado to visit her parents. One evening she sat in the dining car near a man in a distinctive checkered suit. She struck up a conversation with him, and he was so impressed by what he learned about her that he offered her a job. The man was Frederick Bonfils, one of the owners of the *Post*.

Polly was the first woman to work as a reporter for the newspaper, and she had to endure some prejudice from her colleagues. Nonetheless, she quickly made Polly Pry a household name in Colorado. One of her first assignments was to investigate squalid conditions at the state's public institutions. The headline over her exposé screamed, "Our Insane Treatment of the Insane."

Next, as part of a crusade for penal reform, she investigated the state prison in Canon City. A tall, slender, sad-eyed inmate captured her attention, and prison officials identified him as Alfred Packer, a notorious killer and convicted cannibal. Packer and five other prospectors had ventured into the mountains of western Colorado in 1873. They lost their way during a ferocious blizzard and ran out of provisions. Packer was the only one to survive the ordeal. He claimed his comrades had starved to death, but when searchers discovered the bodies of the men, they soon determined that the prospectors had been murdered and parts of them had been eaten. Packer was convicted of the crimes and sentenced to forty years in prison.

Packer refused to talk to the prison warden and guards about the horrible incident, but Polly knew a titillating story when she saw one. She persisted in requesting an interview and ultimately succeeded.

"You understand that was a long time ago," Packer told her. "My liberty was taken away from me. . . . I am innocent of the hideous crime with which I am charged."

Polly believed Packer was guilty not of murder but only of cannibalism—long considered an acceptable practice in desperate times on the high seas. She believed that Packer's circumstances had been equally desperate and began lobbying to get him pardoned. The *Post* was considering hiring attorney W. W. Anderson to appeal his case.

Unbeknownst to the owners of the *Post,* Anderson talked Packer into paying him twenty-five dollars on top of the fee the newspaper would pay him. Packer had received the money as part of his government pension for working as a scout on the plains. When Tammen and Bonfils discovered that Anderson was trying to double-dip, they confronted him—and set off the violent chain of events that almost led to their deaths.

Meanwhile, Polly's sensational news stories about Packer were rankling Colorado officials. They considered the man to be a cold-blooded killer who belonged behind bars, but they were besieged by demands for his release from folks who'd been riled up by Polly's stories. In addition to dedicating many of her news articles to the case, she circulated petitions demanding Packer's release. She even talked such Denver dignitaries as the mayor and police chief into joining her cause.

Colorado Governor Charles S. Thomas finally capitulated in 1901. Polly asked readers to welcome back into society the man once accused of cannibalism. "Let Packer forget the unholy events of the past . . . refrain from epithets [such] as 'man-eater, human hyena and ghoul!'"

One of Polly's next campaigns was to cover labor strife in Colorado's silver-mining camps. Miners and their unions were battling for higher wages and better working conditions. Because women were banned from the mines, she once disguised herself as a man to go underground for a firsthand look.

Polly suggested in her news stories that the Western Federation of Miners, one of the more radical unions of the day, was responsible for several murders. When union leaders organized a boycott of the *Post,* Bonfils began to have misgivings about Polly's aggressive reporting.

Under increasing pressure from editors, Polly decided to resign and start her own weekly newsmagazine, the *Polly Pry.* She billed it as a journal of comment and criticism, but mostly it was a platform for her social theories. Denver, she announced in her first edition, was "just big enough and just lively enough and just naughty enough to need a weekly paper of its own as desperately as a lively boy needs his Saturday night tubbing." For four dollars a year, readers got "something we all need and get mighty little of—and that is a dose of that unpalatable and evanescent bug-a-bear known as the truth," she proclaimed.

Polly's paper teemed with local society gossip, digs at Colorado dignitaries, and her never-ending crusade against the leaders of the Western Federation of Miners. After visiting one mining camp, she reported, "I was there last week and not one day passed without its murders, killings and assaults. . . . The anarchists and socialists of the entire country are making a desperate effort to establish their headquarters in Colorado."

Such bare-knuckles reporting tended to inspire animosity. Late on the evening of January 16, 1904, Polly heard the doorbell chime at her house and office on West Colfax Avenue. Later, she described what happened next:

I went to the front door and some instinct or fear or apprehension made me step behind it—otherwise I would not be writing this—as I swung it open. I looked around the door, and instantly two shots were fired. . . . I saw a long red flame, caught a fleeting glimpse of a big man in dark clothes, and a derby hat; had an instantaneous impression of a dark moustache and a side face marred by a red mark. . . . For the past seven weeks I have been in almost daily receipt of anonymous letters, warning me that I would have to stop attacking union men in my paper or be killed and my office blown to atoms.

When the Denver police investigated, they found bullet holes in Polly's desk and wall. Despite the attack, Polly wrote, "I am going to keep right on running my magazine and writing what I think proper. I have not been attacking union labor, but I have been showing up some of the leaders."

Denver residents rallied to her aid. Newsboys kept an eye out for suspicious people, and the police chief stationed men around her house at night. The governor offered the assistance of the militia.

Polly published her paper for two more years before selling it and taking a prestigious job as Colorado's commissioner for the World's Fair. But soon she found that she missed the thrill of a good scoop and accepted an offer to report for the *Rocky Mountain News*. In 1910 she married again—this time a Denver attorney named Harry O'Bryan—but she didn't let the relationship stand in the way of a good story. She continued to take reporting assignments far from home. In 1914, while traveling to Mexico to write about the daring rebel leader Pancho Villa, she learned that her husband had died.

She could do little for him back in Denver, she decided, so she continued on to Mexico.

When Polly finally interviewed Pancho Villa, he raged about the United States and its meddling in Mexican affairs. "The day may come when I shall have to fight all foreigners and Coloradans, too!" he shouted.

"But not an American woman," she replied, smiling sweetly. "Not a woman who has come all this way to see you."

His grim face broke into a grin. "Never!"

While in Mexico, Polly reported events that few other American journalists ever witnessed. She saw the fall of Torreon, hangings in public squares, and massacres committed by all sides. Once she left a plaza just a few minutes before a bomb exploded, wounding and killing dozens of people. She later said, "I went about unarmed and alone at times among that hostile and war-infested country, among a primitive and semi-civilized people more than two-thirds of whom were Indians. . . . But I was accepted and the rebel officers invited me to make myself at home."

One Mexican official was so amazed to see her amidst the carnage that he reportedly exclaimed, "It is incredible what the American ladies can do!"

Polly's thirst for adventure was still strong at the outbreak of World War I. Though she was in her sixties by then, she sailed to Greece and Albania to work as a volunteer for the American Red Cross. She wired home colorful dispatches describing life in the war-torn countries.

The editors of *Redbook* magazine were so fascinated by Polly that they named her one of the country's five most interesting women. People who met her were struck by how fearless this figure of femininity could be. Her sister-in-law, Annette Campbell of Denver, once told a reporter, "I always thought Polly had a very masculine mind—that is, she thought as a man—though she was very feminine." Gene Fowler, a Colorado author who once worked with Polly and wrote about her exploits in his book *Timber Line,* described her as a "great and tender character with courage unbounded."

When Polly returned to Colorado after the war, she kept busy helping orphans and writing her memoirs, *My Life as a Reporter.* Unfortunately, she suffered a heart attack in July 1938 and never completed the book. Instead, she reluctantly entered Denver's St. Joseph Hospital, where she let it be known that she couldn't afford to be wasting her time. "I must be up," she told a nurse who came to check on her. A few days later, Polly died at the age of eighty-one.

"Yes, she was conscious that there were still stories to be scooped," said one of her newspaper colleagues, Pinky Wayne, "and even in death she ached to be first on the scene."

ANN BASSETT

(1878–1956)

JOSIE BASSETT

(ca. 1874–1964)

CATTLE-RUSTLING QUEENS

Ann Bassett had good reason to fear for her life. The owner of a small ranch in northwestern Colorado, she had watched for decades as trouble brewed between homesteaders and cattle barons over control of the open range. In 1900 two good friends had been murdered, one of them after finding a death threat pinned to his front gate. Now, only months later, Ann had received her own menacing, unsigned letter. It warned her to "leave that country for parts unknown within thirty days or you will be killed."

Ann and her friends figured they knew who was responsible for the letter, as well as for the mounting atrocities: the big cattle companies, which wanted to intimidate settlers into leaving the area so they could seize control of the grazing land and watering holes for their livestock. Ann was frightened, of course, but she was also stubborn. She refused to flee the state and instead avenged her friends' deaths by patrolling the range and killing any cattle from the big outfits that strayed into Brown's Park, where she and her neighbors lived and grazed their herds.

Eventually, the cattle corporations tried a different tactic. In 1911 they pressured the local sheriff into arresting Ann for rustling their cattle. The evidence was flimsy, and public sentiment was decidedly in favor of outspoken Ann, who made no secret of her belief that the "grasping cattle barons . . . were the biggest cattle thieves of all time."

Ann Bassett Denver Public Library, Western History Collection, Z-153

In Craig, where the trial was to be held, townsfolk chipped in to rent the local opera house so more spectators could cram inside to listen to the proceedings. Ann was called to the stand as the final witness for the defense.

"Her hourglass figure beautifully dressed, her rich brown hair perfectly coiffed, [she] presented a picture of a maligned and abused lady being persecuted by evil men," according to biographer Grace McClure.

The trial ended in a hung jury. A second trial two years later ended in Ann's acquittal. Many westerners were ecstatic that she had won her feud with the powerful cattle barons. "Businesses Close, Bands Blare— Town of Craig Goes Wild with Joy!" screamed the headline in the *Denver Post*. Ann was "placed in an automobile and paraded through the main streets of the town receiving the congratulations and well wishes of her friends," according to the story that followed.

But many people, including some of Ann's friends, harbored no doubt that she *had* rustled a few cattle in her lifetime. No one protested—not even Ann—when a Denver reporter dubbed her the "Queen of the Cattle Rustlers." For the rest of her life she was proud to be known as "Queen Ann." The title paid homage to her showdown with the cattle barons, as well as to her regal bearing and imperious presence.

Ann wasn't the only Bassett who could lay claim to being a legend. Her mother, Elizabeth, founded the family ranch and ran it successfully at a time when ranching was considered a man's domain. Ann's sister Josie entered local lore as a gun-toting, self-sufficient pioneer who married and discarded five husbands, one of them under suspicious circumstances.

No more appropriate place could the hardy Bassett clan call home than Brown's Park, a thirty-five-mile-long valley that straddles the border between northwestern Colorado and northeastern Utah. Isolated and sparsely populated, the area was a magnet for outlaws on the run in the late 1800s. Some, including Butch Cassidy, became fast friends

Josie Bassett Uintah County Library Regional History Center

of the Bassetts. As McClure said in her entertaining 1985 book *The Bassett Women*:

> *In this rustlers' hangout, surrounded by warring cattlemen, the Bassetts lived in a world of rustling and thievery, of lynching and other forms of murder. Their neighbors could constitute the standard cast of a Hollywood western: honest ranchers, rough and tough cowboys, worthless drifters, dastardly villains, sneaking rustlers, gentlemanly bank robbers, desperate outlaws, and ruthless cattle barons. Most Americans assume this world vanished long ago, yet people alive today remember Queen Ann striding along in her custom-made boots and Josie riding to town for supplies with her team and wagon.*

Even though flanked by other fascinating frontier characters, the Bassett women commanded attention. They expected to be treated as men's equals—not because they wanted to change social mores, but because they believed that the freedom offered by the West was as much theirs as any man's. According to McClure, they had "audacity and strong will, high temper and obstinacy, good humor and openhandedness, unashamed sexuality—qualities that their contemporaries summed up as 'the Bassett charm.'"

Originally from Arkansas, the Bassett family migrated west in 1877 in search of a drier climate that would offer Herb, the sickly family patriarch, some relief from his asthma. They settled in Brown's Park, where Herb's brother Sam had been prospecting for more than twenty years. They soon discovered that the country, while handsome and invigorating, offered no instant riches.

Cattle fever was sweeping the West, and ambitious Elizabeth was soon infected. Cattle ranching, she believed, was her ticket to prosperity. Once she built a herd, she could fatten her livestock for free on thousands of square miles of public grasslands that until recently had supported buffalo.

However, there were risks to the cattle business. While lawmen turned a blind eye, rich and greedy cattle barons were snatching up what public grazing land they could, and many of them had no compunction about running off small ranchers and homesteaders who got in their way. Any settler who tried to fight back risked seeing his cabin and crops go up in flames. Worse yet, he might be lynched or shot in the back. But so far the cattle barons had shown little interest in the remote meadows of Brown's Park. So while Herb, a "little old maid of a man," served first as the local postmaster and then as justice of the peace, Elizabeth began building her herd.

The Bassetts also continued to build their family. Their first two children, Josie and Samuel, had been born in Arkansas. In 1878 Ann became the first known white child born in Brown's Park. A second Bassett son, Elbert, was born a year later. Elizabeth didn't have enough breast milk to nourish infant Ann, so she employed a Ute Indian mother as a wet nurse. Six months later, a family friend presented Ann with a milk cow.

"I got into the cow business at a decidedly early age," she later joked.

Ann did start cowboying early in life. At the age of six, she was herding cattle on horseback.

"I had the privilege of living in a bronco West," she later said. "My ambitions were centered upon an ability to flank a calf or stick a wild cow's head through a loop, as neatly as any of them."

When young Ann rode the range, fences were as rare as ships in the mountains. Cattle wandered far and wide, and there weren't enough cowboys to keep track of them. Ranchers expected to lose some animals to bad weather and predators, but they could not abide rustlers, who were experts at altering brands and rounding up unbranded mavericks.

In McClure's opinion, a certain amount of rustling was to be expected, perhaps even excused, given the "conditions under which [settlers] were struggling to survive."

"These illegal brandings . . . are as understandable as a slum kid's snitching an apple from a grocer's pile of fruit," she wrote.

Still, when rumors began to circulate that Elizabeth was building her herd by branding strays and buying cut-rate cattle from professional rustlers, one stockman disdainfully declared her the head of the "Bassett gang."

One of Elizabeth's ranch hands was Butch Cassidy, a good-natured young man who loved to read books from Herb's extensive library. Sometimes Cassidy went dancing with fifteen-year-old Josie on his arm. She once referred to him as her "Brown's Park beau," though in later years she coyly refused to confirm or deny any relationship. Ann adored Cassidy, too. As an eleven-year-old, she tailed him like a puppy as he did his chores.

A neighbor once saw the Bassett sisters get into a "knock-down, drag-out" fight as they argued over Cassidy's affections. In her late teens, Ann was a close companion of Cassidy, holing up with him at the "Robbers Roost" hideout across the Utah border. Meanwhile, Josie had relationships with two other members of the Wild Bunch, Elzy Lay, Cassidy's closest friend, and Will "News" Carver.

Back on the Bassett ranch, Elizabeth honed her considerable skills as a rancher. While blizzards in the winters of 1885 and 1887 destroyed bigger operations, her herd emerged as strong as ever. Her luck finally played out in 1892, when she apparently suffered either a miscarriage or appendicitis and died at the age of thirty-seven. The Bassetts had lost their anchor—and their main source of income.

Ann and Josie, still teenagers, had to grow up quickly to survive on the unforgiving frontier. They managed in part because of their friendships with the Wild Bunch, which kept at bay the wealthy cattlemen who lusted after their land. Ann's seven-year, off-and-on relationship with

Cassidy ended at the turn of the twentieth century, when the famous gang leader fled for South America.

Josie found the years after her mother's death especially trying. In 1894 she married Jim McKnight, one of three hands who had helped Elizabeth run the Bassett ranch. When McKnight, a longtime bachelor, began visiting a nearby saloon to escape the constraints of matrimony, Josie fumed. When McKnight proposed leaving their ranch, moving to Vernal, and opening a saloon of their own, Josie filed for divorce. She was not about to let a man come between her and her love of ranch life.

In April 1900 the conflict came to a head when a sheriff's deputy tried to serve McKnight with divorce papers. As strong willed and hot tempered as his wife, he refused to accept them and walked away. The deputy ordered McKnight to halt, then shot and badly wounded him when he refused.

Josie's second marriage lasted four years, and her third just six months. She tried to cure her fourth husband, Emerson Wells, of a drinking problem by feeding him a medicine known as the Keeley Cure, and he died suddenly after a New Year Eve's binge. Because of her checkered reputation, Josie was accused by gossipmongers of poisoning Wells, but there was no proof and she was never charged with a crime.

Now thirty-nine years old, Josie decided to homestead just over the Colorado-Utah border, at Cub Creek near Vernal. She made another bad choice in mates—a rude, crude man named Morris. After her new husband abused her horse, Josie chased him off with a frying pan.

Josie was a hard worker but always found it difficult to make ends meet. In the 1920s Prohibition offered her an enticing opportunity. She was not a drinker herself, but she had no qualms about making her living selling moonshine. She set up a still in the gulch below her cabin and brewed corn whiskey and apricot brandy for the next several years, guaranteeing herself a steady source of income. Finally, her family prevailed on her to stop before she ended up in jail.

Though she had little money, Josie was always willing to help neighbors who had less than she did. She regularly loaded poached venison or rustled beef into her wagon and delivered it to hungry families.

"It is almost surprising that it was not until January 1936 that she was indicted for stealing cattle belonging to the ranchers who grazed their cattle" near her homestead, according to McClure. Josie was tried twice for rustling, but despite strong evidence, the compassionate grandmother was acquitted both times. She once explained how she escaped a conviction when she went to trial:

I put on a frilly print dress, and sensible shoes, and had my hair done in a domestic roll on the top of my head. I looked like a petite little middle-aged housewife as I stood before the judge. Putting on my best serious face, I said to him, "Your Honor, do you seriously believe that a little old lady weighing only 100 pounds could kill and butcher out even one beef cow by herself, let alone a dozen or more? If you can believe that, then I guess you will have to find me guilty."

Even in her seventies, Josie pushed the boundaries of the law. She once got fed up with a neighbor's mule that had pestered her horses and killed her granddaughter's colt. So she lured the mule into the hills, shot it, and sent it tumbling to the bottom of a gully.

Life magazine learned of Josie's exploits and dispatched reporters to investigate in 1948. The resulting story depicted Josie as a salty, rifle-toting frontierswoman. It also called her the "Queen of the Cattle Rustlers," much to Ann's chagrin. The article inspired a 1967 movie, *The Ballad of Josie,* starring Doris Day.

Ann got her own moment in the media spotlight when she detailed her colorful life in articles in *Colorado Magazine* in 1952 and 1953. With a penchant for elaboration, she didn't make it easy for readers to sort fact from fiction. In one story she claimed she roped a grizzly cub when she was just thirteen. The enraged grizzly sow chased Ann up a tree, she said, and then mauled her horse. Cowboys rode to the rescue and shot the mother bear, then gave Ann "the damnedest shaking" and licking a kid could ever get, she reported.

Ann spent part of her childhood at boarding schools in Salt Lake City and Boston, where she learned to appreciate culture. The tough tomboy who could bust a bronc could also quote Shakespeare. In fact, the Bassett home brimmed with books that included the complete works of Shakespeare, as well as volumes by Keats, Byron, Longfellow, Shelley, and Dickens.

"In the end she became a genuine curiosity," according to Colorado historians John H. Monnett and Michael McCarthy, "a frontier hybrid of both toughness and beauty, part poet, but part hellion too, who smelled at once of damp leather and eastern perfume, and who at all times remained an enigma to those around her."

When Ann was twenty-six, she shocked friends and foes alike by propositioning a cowboy named Hi Bernard, who was twenty years her senior. It wasn't so much the age difference that set tongues wagging; it was the fact that Bernard worked for the Bassetts' archrival, Ora Haley, a cattle baron who owned the immense Two-Bar Ranch. Many folks, including Ann, believed that Haley had ordered the murders of two of the Bassetts' friends and neighbors. Still, Ann knew Bernard was one of the best cowmen in the country, and she needed his help to expand her own cattle business. Not surprisingly, Haley's wedding gift to Bernard was the frontier equivalent of a pink slip.

Young Ann soon became bored with her new husband. She started spending time in the company of a handsome cowboy, and Bernard moved to Denver. Ann later divorced him and married Frank Willis, an easygoing man who could tolerate her hot temper and freewheeling ways. When Ann knocked him out with a frying pan for coming home drunk one night, he simply shrugged off the incident.

Ann spent her days running the family ranch, mingling with outlaws, and repelling the cattle barons who tried to take over her land. She continued to live a hard and fast-paced life until 1953, when she suffered a severe heart attack. She died three years later, on May 8, 1956, at the age of seventy-eight.

Shortly before her death, she told a reporter, "I've done everything they said I did and a helluva lot more."

Josie continued to live alone at her homestead on Cub Creek, where there was no running water, electricity, or telephone. She spent fifty years in her cabin there and left at the age of eighty-nine, after suffering a broken hip when her horse knocked her down. Realizing she'd never be able to return home, she died in May 1964 at a Salt Lake City hospital.

Josie was buried near Ann and Elizabeth on the family homestead at Brown's Park. She was the last Bassett to be interred there. The family plot is not open to the public, but tourists can visit Josie's homestead and cabin at Dinosaur National Monument.

Josie and Ann both lived long enough to see the end of the frontier, but they stubbornly refused to change with the times. They never abandoned the spirit and the values they acquired on their homesteads. As McClure put it:

> Both women [carried] a combination of pioneer values and an utter disregard for any conventions that ran counter to their own standards of right and wrong. They were sometimes condemned by their more conservative contemporaries—understandably, for what they did was not always admirable. They lived their lives as they wished, doing what they wanted to do or what they felt they were compelled to do, with never a serious qualm when they overstepped the bounds of a "proper society."

Margaret Tobin Brown

(1867–1932)
DAUGHTER OF ADVENTURE

Shortly before midnight on her third night at sea, Margaret Tobin Brown was curled in the brass bed of her elegant stateroom, deeply engrossed in a good book. Suddenly, the massive steamship gave a jolt, tumbling her to the floor. Startled but not frightened, she got to her feet, slipped a dressing gown over her nightclothes, and ventured into the corridor.

A handful of curious passengers and crew loitered nearby, chatting and joking with one another. Margaret noticed that the engines of the luxury liner had stopped their incessant throbbing. All was eerily silent, but nothing seemed amiss. She returned to her bed and resumed reading. A few minutes later, she heard a clamor in the gangway and went to investigate again.

"I saw a man whose face was blanched, his eyes protruding, wearing the look of a haunted creature," she later wrote. "He was grasping for breath, and in an undertone he gasped, 'Get your life-saver!'"

Margaret rushed back to her room and slipped into the warmest clothing she could find: a black velvet two-piece suit, seven pairs of woolen stockings, and a sable stole. She took five hundred dollars from her room safe, tucked it into a small wallet, and strapped on her life jacket. Then she hurried up to the top deck of the *Titanic*, where knots of passengers buzzed with the news: The ship, on its maiden voyage from England to New York, had rammed an iceberg and was taking on water. Some of the crew began to lower the lifeboats.

As a young woman, Margaret had held her own in the tough, male-dominated mining town of Leadville, Colorado. She was not easily

Margaret Tobin Brown Denver Public Library, Western History Collection, X-21980

intimidated, and she saw no reason to panic now. The *Titanic*, after all, had been widely hailed by the press as a "floating palace" that could not possibly sink because of its revolutionary double-bottomed hull and watertight bulkheads. Even if the ship did go down, Margaret figured, she was a strong swimmer. And surely help would arrive soon. Amid the din and confusion, she calmly helped other women and children into the lifeboats until she felt someone lift her from behind.

"I would probably be at the bottom of the fathomless sea were it not for the two powerful men who picked me up like a child and dropped me into the lowering lifeboat," she later recalled.

Margaret was one of two dozen passengers in lifeboat six, the first to pull away from the port side of the *Titanic* on that fateful night of April 14, 1912. The little boat was meant to hold sixty-five people, but, like most of the lifeboats on the Titanic, it was only partially filled in the rush to escape the sinking ship. Quartermaster Robert Hichens, one of the few men to jump aboard, took charge.

"Row as hard as you can!" he shouted. "We need to get away from the suction! She's so large that when she sinks, she'll pull everything down for miles around."

Margaret strained at the oars, helping to maneuver around floating chunks of ice, until a great rumbling noise drew her attention back to the *Titanic*. She and the other occupants of the lifeboat watched in silence and horror as the ship rose at the stern and seemed to break in two. The next image she saw seared itself into her soul.

"Suddenly there was a rift in the water, the sea opened up, and the surface foamed like giant arms that spread around the ship," she later recalled. The *Titanic* slid beneath the surface and disappeared.

The starry night filled with a cacophony of terror—the anguished wails and shouts of hundreds of men, women, and children as they floundered in the frigid sea.

"We have to go back!" Margaret cried. "We can't leave them!"

But Hichens refused to change course. "We would go to our own deaths!" he argued. "They would only pull us down. Row! Row!"

Hichens's cowardice infuriated Margaret, but she resumed paddling. She urged her fellow passengers to row harder, realizing that they needed to exert themselves to avoid hypothermia. Some sources say the boat did go back that night, at Margaret's insistence, and the occupants did rescue more survivors from the sea. The details will forever remain shrouded in the fog of that tragic night.

Meanwhile, six long, miserable hours passed before the occupants of the lifeboat spotted the *Carpathia* steaming to the rescue. Margaret's body was weak and aching as she climbed aboard the ship, but she refused to rest. Fluent in several foreign languages—and the daughter of Irish immigrants herself—she comforted immigrant passengers, handed out blankets, and compiled a list of survivors so that officials could notify their relatives. Then she organized a drive to raise ten thousand dollars to help immigrant survivors who had lost everything—not only family, but clothes, money, and valuables—on their way to a new life in the New World. Immigration law prohibited penniless foreigners from remaining in America, and some of the survivors were terrified that they would be sent back to their homelands.

When the *Carpathia* docked in New York City, Margaret was greeted by family members eager to whisk her off to a hot meal and a warm bed. But she insisted on staying until arrangements had been made for the very last of the *Titanic* survivors.

Margaret's heroics caught the attention of reporters who were seeking any possible scrap of good news from the tragedy that had claimed close to 1,500 lives.

"They are petitioning Congress to give me a medal and to inscribe my name on the monument erected in New York harbor," she wrote to her daughter Helen. "If I must call a specialist to examine my head it is due to the title of Heroine of the *Titanic*."

As tales of her role in the disaster spread, Margaret became one of the most enduring folk legends of the twentieth century, her story kept alive by countless articles, books, a Broadway play, and two popular movies: *The Unsinkable Molly Brown* and *Titanic*. But the more often her story was repeated, the more fact and fiction merged. Even her name was altered. Although she was always known to friends and family as Margaret, or Maggie, Hollywood chose to call her Molly Brown.

Margaret was never too concerned about the distortions. Flamboyant and theatrical, she herself was known as a "bit of a confabulator." She loved to tell stories, perform, and bask in the spotlight. If a writer told a whopper that made her story more interesting, well, who was she to complain?

A relative once asked her why she didn't correct a report that her husband had accidentally burned up $300,000 in cash that she had stashed in their potbellied stove.

"It's a damn good story," she reportedly replied. "And I don't care what the newspapers say about me, just so they say something."

In her book, *Molly Brown: Denver's Unsinkable Lady*, author Christine Whitacre described Margaret this way:

> [She] loved publicity and her active imagination and theatrical flair helped perpetuate such stories. They became more exaggerated after her death. And the 1960s Broadway musical and Hollywood movie that glamorized her life—even if they did gloss over her considerable personal difficulties—finally succeeded in making her name a household word. But Margaret Brown's life did not have to be fictionalized to be made interesting. She was a remarkable woman.

Margaret might have described her life as a rags-to-riches story. She was born in Hannibal, Missouri, on July 18, 1867, to Irish immigrants.

Margaret Brown in one of her flamboyant outfits Denver Public Library, Western History Collection, X-21702

Her father, John Tobin, worked for the local gas company, while her mother, Johanna, raised the couple's six children. Almost a century later, after Margaret had become a celebrity, author Gene Fowler claimed that she had befriended Hannibal's most famous resident, Mark Twain.

"He at once saw her for what she was, a female Huckleberry Finn," Fowler wrote in his 1933 book *Timber Line*.

Although the description of her may have been apt, Margaret probably never met Twain. He had left Hannibal fourteen years before she was born. Perhaps, though, she knew his books and was drawn to the West by his tales of adventure and opportunity there.

Margaret moved to Leadville in 1886, apparently because her brother, half-sister, and brother-in-law lived there. She took a job as a clerk in a dry-goods store. Full-figured, red-haired, and vivacious, she undoubtedly turned heads, since men far outnumbered women in the bustling mining town. A coworker once wrote that Margaret was "exceptionally bright, a most interesting conversationalist, had a charming personality and this coupled with her beauty made her a very attractive woman."

One of her admirers was J. J. Brown, an ambitious miner from Pennsylvania. Margaret liked J. J., too, but she had reservations. According to Kristen Iversen's thorough biography, *Molly Brown: Unraveling the Myth*:

> *Maggie couldn't help but dream of marrying a man wealthy enough to help her and her family out of their straitened circumstances. But despite her adamant intentions, she fell instead for a man whose situation was scarcely different from her own. James Joseph Brown was a tall, personable young Irishman, and—like Maggie—intelligent, gregarious, and very ambitious. He was smitten with the auburn-haired Irish girl he first met at a Catholic picnic. But he was poor.*

Margaret eventually put aside her misgivings and married Brown on September 18, 1886, just months after the couple first met. He was thirty-two and she was nineteen. Determined to better educate herself, she began to study literature and music. A son, Lawrence, was born the following year, and Helen arrived two years later. The Brown home grew even more crowded as many of Margaret's relatives moved to Colorado from Missouri. Margaret didn't mind; family was important to her. She considered those early Leadville years as among the happiest of her life.

Life also smiled on J. J. He rapidly rose through the ranks at the Leadville silver mines to become superintendent of Henriette and Maid Consolidated Mining, and then a partner in the Ibex Mining Company. Just as silver prices crashed in 1893, he discovered gold in Ibex's Little Jonny Mine and ingeniously used hay bales and timbers to shore up the sandy mine shaft. He was paid handsomely for his innovation. The extra money allowed him to move his family out of Leadville, where winters could be as cold as arctic ice caps, and into a $30,000 mansion in Denver's upscale Capitol Hill district.

Margaret, now twenty-seven, was eager to become part of Denver's social elite. But, according to legend, city socialites spurned her for being too coarse, too Irish, and too Catholic. As with many myths, the story holds a grain of truth. A group called "the Sacred 36"—the top layer of Denver's upper crust—did pointedly exclude Margaret from their activities for many years. A local gossip newspaper called *Polly Pry* mocked her for a lack of good breeding, for trying too hard to be accepted, and for pretentiously naming her new lodge near Denver the *Avoca,* a word borrowed from a Thomas Moore poem. Margaret plaintively wrote the paper, "May I be pardoned of so grave a crime?" *Polly Pry* used the letter to poke fun at her again; the paper ran it verbatim with its many misspellings and awkward phrases.

These incidents notwithstanding, press clippings from the period show that Margaret was no social outcast. As author Iversen pointed out, "From 1894 to the early 1920s, the Browns took up more space in Denver's society pages than nearly any other Denver family and were regularly listed on the Social Register. Margaret and J. J. were not ostracized by Denver society—they *were* Denver society."

Margaret loved to host dinners and other soirees and was frequently invited to social events. She and J. J. were regular patrons of opera and theater. She even developed a reputation as a trendsetter and was asked to model the latest fashions for newspaper photographers. One society page photo showed her in a lace dress festooned with ermine and gold embroidery. It was described as one of the most elaborate dresses ever assembled; it took three months to create.

"Perhaps no woman in society has ever spent more time or money becoming 'civilized' than has Mrs. Brown," reported the *Denver Post* at the time.

Margaret had not gone to all this effort just to gratify herself. She cared about the community, and she used her stature and influence to promote many causes. As a Leadville resident, she campaigned for education reforms and organized a soup kitchen for impoverished families. In Denver one of her pet projects was River Front Park, a playground and summer school for some five hundred low-income children. She also spearheaded efforts to expand St. Joseph Hospital and construct the Cathedral of the Immaculate Conception.

Margaret "is a woman of large philanthropic interests and meets every request for aid with generous response," noted a 1914 book, *Representative Women of Colorado*.

Like other reform-minded women, Margaret pursued many of her interests through women's clubs, which typically advocated better schools, women's suffrage, poverty programs, and an end to alcoholism and prostitution. She joined forces with Judge Benjamin Lindsey, a nationally recognized juvenile justice reformer, and regularly sponsored fundraisers. She even reopened an abandoned gold mine to raise money for his cause.

"The juveniles of Judge Lindsey's court have had no better friend than Mrs. Brown," a Colorado newspaper declared.

Margaret plunged wholeheartedly into political causes, among them the fight for equal rights for women. She believed that, in their quest for equality, women should expect to share all civic responsibilities, even military service. She once proposed that the United States dispatch a regiment of female soldiers to Mexico if tensions there erupted into war. Her idea was widely scorned—by women as well as men.

Still, Margaret won converts who admired her willingness to speak out and challenge conventions of the day. Even *Polly Pry*, the reformist newspaper that had once mocked her, eventually became a supporter of her reform efforts.

In 1914 Margaret demonstrated the courage that had held her in good stead on the *Titanic* by taking on the titans of Colorado's mining industry. After militiamen murdered children and women during the Ludlow coal strike in southern Colorado, she organized relief efforts for miners' families and demanded that working conditions be improved. She once said that getting money from rich people to help the poor was the highlight of her life.

"I suppose there are some persons who would like me to sit down to devote the rest of my life to bridge," she said. "Times have changed, and there's no reason why I should, like my mother at forty, put on my glasses and do little but read."

Several times Margaret launched campaigns for public office to give her a platform from which to promote her policies. And she had many backers. The *Washington* (DC) *Pathfinder* once endorsed her, hailing her as an "out-and-out, patriotic American." In 1901 Margaret ran for a state Senate seat but withdrew before the election. Thirteen years later she announced her candidacy for the US Senate. However, she put the campaign on hold when she was asked to go to Europe to serve as director of the American Committee for Devastated France. In that job, she managed ambulance drivers and oversaw the distribution of aid in war-ravaged villages. Her work in Europe not only forced her to abandon the 1914 race, but it made her give up the notion of running in Colorado's 1916 Senate contest, too. In 1932 Margaret was recognized by the French Legion of Honor for her humanitarian efforts during the war, as well as for assisting Titanic survivors.

J.J. was appalled by Margaret's outspokenness and involvement in civic affairs. He thought women belonged at home, seen but not heard. He also resented his wife's frequent trips to Europe, her extravagant spending habits, and the way she spoiled their children and turned them against him. He once grumbled that Margaret had "ruined" their children "for any earthly use." On another occasion he complained to his son, "Your mother is my greatest enemy."

Margaret had reason to be upset with J. J., too. She had heard rumors of his philandering, and she was horribly embarrassed in 1904, when a Denver man sued J.J. for seducing his twenty-two-year-old wife. In 1909, after twenty-three years of marriage, Margaret and J.J. separated. J.J. agreed to give Margaret their Denver mansion and monthly support payments of seven hundred dollars.

Who was responsible for the breakup? As is often the case, there was plenty of blame to go around, but daughter Helen believed that her mother's quest for fame and influence was the biggest factor. Margaret "was not entirely to blame in the trouble with father, not originally, because he was difficult, hot tempered in the extreme and hard to please," Helen said. "But whereas he tried and did mend his ways and controlled himself more and more as he grew older . . . she succumbed more and more to what became . . . a ruling passion in her life."

As the chasm between J. J. and Margaret widened, she spent more time at the family's forty-three-room cottage in Newport, Rhode Island. She also delighted in traveling to Switzerland, Italy, Egypt, India, and other exotic places. In the spring of 1912, while visiting Paris, she learned that her infant grandson was extremely ill. Eager to be with him, she bought a ticket for home—on the *Titanic.*

As the years passed, J. J.'s fortune dwindled, and Margaret was forced to economize. She fretted over this and over his failing health; she still had feelings for her husband. He died on September 5, 1922, leaving an estate worth $238,000 but no will that spelled out its disposition. Margaret accused her children of hiding an additional $200,000 from the estate and filed a lawsuit to get a bigger share. After years of wrangling, a judge settled the fracas by putting $100,000 in trust for Margaret, another $100,000 in trust for her two children, and splitting the remaining property equally. The "hidden" $200,000 he allowed the children to keep.

Margaret was so livid over the ruling that she stopped communicating with her children and cut them from her will. So, like everyone else in the country, Helen and Lawrence kept track of their mother's escapades by reading the newspapers. She still drew headlines, attracting reporters the way royalty draws paparazzi. One 1925 news story reported that she led fellow guests down a fire escape when flames broke out in a Florida hotel. There were other stories that Margaret planned to adopt a child and marry an English duke. She quickly squelched the wedding rumor.

"Me marry that old geezer?" she scoffed. "Never! Give me every time the rugged men of the West."

Occasionally, the news about Margaret was more flattering. In 1929 newspapers reported that France had awarded her the Palm of the Academy in honor of her interpretive stage portrayal of actress Sarah Bernhardt, and in 1932 news broke of her French Legion of Honor award. In America she drew accolades for restoring the Denver home of Eugene Fields, author of "Wynken, Blynken, and Nod" and other children's poems.

But the favorable press could not hide an unpleasant fact. As Margaret moved into her sixties, she became more erratic and eccentric.

Friends and relatives worried that she would soon be unable to care for herself.

While visiting Denver from Newport in 1930, she strutted down the street in a purple silk dress, a feather boa, and a pink-plumed hat. A *Denver Post* reporter saw that she

> *had great dignity. There was something terribly regal about her. Perhaps it was her tall, gold-tipped swagger stick, or the way she peered through the lorgnettes on a gold chain about her bulging neck. Perhaps it was the way she gazed over my head as she strutted pompously, though with faltering steps, down 17th Street, like a Civil War veteran. Heads turned at the sight of her, and as she passed by, she left in a wake an essence of violets, rose-water and mothballs. Everything about her was amazing and fascinating. I sensed that she was a brave and lonely woman probably living in the heyday of her past.*

Margaret eventually moved to New York City, where she lived at the Barbizon Hotel. There, on October 26, 1932, she died at the age of sixty-five. The death certificate reported the cause as a cerebral hemorrhage, but an autopsy uncovered a brain tumor. Her family buried her next to J. J. in a Long Island cemetery not far from the home of their daughter Helen.

Margaret's remarkable life was at an end, but her legend was in its infancy. A year after her death, Fowler's *Timber Line* presented a fanciful account of her exploits. *Reader's Digest* reprinted the story, and a radio show called *The Unsinkable Mrs. Brown* hit the airways. Her legend continued to mushroom when *The Unsinkable Molly Brown* became a Broadway hit and the 1960 movie version featuring Debbie Reynolds filled theaters. Even the federal government got into the act. In the 1950s it portrayed her on savings bonds as a swashbuckling

Titanic survivor. Later, the Gemini 3 spacecraft was unofficially dubbed the "Molly Brown."

In Colorado, Margaret's story has been remembered more accurately. A group called Historic Denver painstakingly restored her Queen Anne–style mansion. It now serves as the Molly Brown House Museum, attracting tens of thousands of visitors a year. There, tourists discover that the real Margaret Tobin Brown is even more fascinating than the Molly Brown they "know" from *Titanic* or *The Unsinkable Molly Brown*.

They learn that Margaret was a woman of many faces. She was a woman of action, compassion, and convictions. She was a woman, one writer said, who had the courage to be herself. Margaret characterized herself as a "daughter of adventure."

"This means I never experience a dull moment and must be prepared for any eventuality," she said.

Perhaps the *Denver Post* summed up Margaret Brown best:

Not being a man, she determined to be a successful woman, to see this world, to meet its best and be one of them. . . . She had a definite, fearless personality. She knew what she wanted and went after it, and seldom failed her goal.

JOSEPHINE ROCHE

(1886–1976)

LABOR ADVOCATE

Hundreds of embittered strikers picketed the Columbine Mine near Lafayette on a brisk fall day in 1927, demanding safer working conditions and higher wages. Suddenly, their shouts were interrupted by the burp of a machine gun that opened fire from atop a water tower. When the racket stopped, six coal miners lay dead and dozens more were wounded.

At her office in Denver, Josephine Roche shuddered when she heard news of the shootings—an echo of the infamous Ludlow Massacre of 1914. As one of the Columbine Mine's biggest shareholders, she knew she had to do something. She rushed to the mine and ordered the guards there to bury their rifles and the machine gun in an abandoned shaft. Then she met with the miners and promised them justice.

As soon as she returned to Denver, Josephine called an emergency meeting of the board of directors of the Rocky Mountain Fuel Company, which owned the mine. Some of the directors berated her for disarming the mine's guards. They worried that the angry workers might seek revenge.

But Josephine refused to back down. A self-professed believer in "humanity over profit," she realized that her best hope of improving conditions at the mine was to become the majority stockholder. So she bought out another owner and hired a company manager who was willing to cooperate with the workers. Promising to "substitute reason for violence, confidence for misunderstanding, integrity and good faith for dishonesty," she invited the United Mine Workers of America into the state, negotiated a union contract, established collective bargaining, and boosted wages to seven dollars a day—the highest in the industry.

Josephine Roche History Colorado, Biographical Portrait File

Josephine wasn't simply being kindhearted. She was an astute business executive who believed that the workers would respond to her gestures of good faith. She was right. Productivity skyrocketed. The company was soon able to bill itself as Colorado's second-biggest producer of coal.

This was neither the first nor the last time that Josephine defied convention. A lifelong social activist who once described her only hobby as "humanity," she battled ignorance and injustice on many fronts. She fought gambling and prostitution as Denver's first policewoman. She campaigned to reform federal child labor laws. She worked to get the downtrodden out of soup lines and into jobs. She became one of the first women to serve in a presidential cabinet and the first to run for governor of Colorado.

"In 1936, Eleanor Roosevelt referred to her as one of America's greatest women," according to Rocky Mountain Fuel executive Gerald Armstrong. "She is a person with spirit, with love, and dedication [who] courageously faced many adversities."

Josephine's background offered little hint of the reformer she would become. She was born into a wealthy family in Neligh, Nebraska, on December 2, 1886. Her father, John Roche, was a prosperous banker and investor who could afford to send his daughter first to Vassar, where she earned a degree in sociology in 1908, and then to Columbia University, where she earned a master's degree in social work in 1910. In her master's thesis, "Economic Conditions in Relation to the Delinquency of Girls," she argued that low wages for women could force them into prostitution.

The Roches moved to Denver in 1906, when John Roche took the helm of Rocky Mountain Fuel. The company had mines in Louisville and west of Denver, as well as in Lafayette.

Even as a youngster, Josephine questioned conditions at the mines. "I was about twelve, and I wanted to go down in a coal mine," she told a reporter for the *Rocky Mountain News* in 1975. "My father said it was too dangerous. I can remember saying, 'If it is too dangerous for me, why isn't it just as dangerous for the men?'"

Josephine first turned her humanitarian instincts into action as a college student, when she did volunteer work with the poor in New York City. She also spent two summers working as an assistant for a juvenile court judge named Benjamin Lindsey. After graduation she got an intriguing offer from Denver Police Commissioner George Creel. He asked her to become the capital city's first female cop.

Josephine jumped at the chance, although it meant patrolling the theaters, saloons, gambling dens, and brothels of Denver's seediest district. As the city's new "inspector of amusements," her charge was to stop the exploitation of vulnerable young women. By all accounts, she did her job well—perhaps too well. She pushed so hard to close Denver's brothels that the Fire and Police Board was bombarded with complaints. The board fired her, alleging that she was hurting the business community.

"My activities on behalf of social betterment were obnoxious to the administration," she later wrote. Josephine appealed to the Civil Service Commission and won back her job, but she had only wanted to make her point. She quit the next day to become a probation officer for Judge Lindsey, who was gaining an international reputation for his juvenile justice reforms. The new position was a good fit. Josephine was an eager convert to the Progressive movement that was sweeping the country in the early 1900s, and in 1914 she became secretary of the Colorado Progressive Party.

That same year, a violent strike at a coal mine in southern Colorado convinced her to expand her crusade for social justice. On the morning of April 20, 1914, National Guard troops opened fire on a tent colony of some 1,200 coal miners and their families at Ludlow. The miners had been protesting their shabby treatment by Colorado Fuel and Iron, a company controlled by the Rockefellers. The soldiers and miners exchanged gunfire into the evening, when the guardsmen torched the colony and burned it to the ground. As many as twenty inhabitants died, including two women and eleven children. The Ludlow Massacre, one of the darkest chapters in American mining history, spawned a national outcry for mining industry reforms.

Josephine rushed to Ludlow to comfort the grief-stricken families. Then she escorted miners' wives to New York City to testify before the US Industrial Relations Commission.

During World War I, Josephine focused her attention and energy on helping the war effort. She served in England as a special agent for the Belgian Relief Committee and then returned to New England to organize the Belgian relief effort. Later, she directed the Foreign Language Information Service, which explained US war policies to the nation's foreign language newspapers. She also served as an editor at the US Children's Bureau and campaigned against child labor in the sugar beet industry. She once attacked industry for its apparent belief that "children are cheaper than machines."

When Josephine's father fell ill in 1925, she returned to Denver. As president of the Rocky Mountain Fuel Company, John Roche had a reputation as a "union-hating" man. When he died in 1927, Josephine inherited his stock and his board seat. She became vice president of the company in 1928 and president in 1929.

This was foreign territory for the social crusader. She was now one of those corporate officials whom she had held in such low regard. But she also recognized that she now had the power to directly benefit her workers. She quickly set out to implement her own progressive policies.

"Labor and management have been misjudged, even persecuted," she said. "Both are right. Big business needs big labor, and both can benefit if each will hear the other."

Josephine's employees responded to her efforts to improve their salaries and working conditions by becoming Colorado's most productive coal miners from 1929 to 1944. Later, when Colorado Fuel and Iron slashed prices and wages in an effort to sink Rocky Mountain Fuel, her workers persuaded their union to loan Roche's firm $80,000 to help keep it afloat. Her company struggled again the following year, and she was forced to cut wages from $7 a day to $5.25, but she offered her miners land to farm and credit at the company store to help them get by.

Although Josephine devoted much of her energy to the company, it wasn't her sole undertaking. In 1934 she challenged Colorado's incumbent governor, Ed Johnson, in the Democratic primary. In a report on the contest, *Literary Digest* noted that Josephine wasn't married—a two-year marriage had ended in divorce in 1920—but she was "distinctly feminine." The article continued:

> *There are none of the usual semimasculine trappings about her, such as flat-heeled shoes, and severely cut clothes. Her movements are quick, almost nervous, but they also are feminine. Her face is framed in soft waves of unbobbed hair: a smile comes readily to her firm lips. Many of her statements are punctuated by a pleasant, slightly nervous laugh. One might apply to her personality such adjectives as forceful, vital, direct.*

In her direct way Josephine campaigned to liberalize Colorado's outdated constitution, reform the tax system, build more highways, and bolster New Deal programs and humanitarian efforts. Her campaign slogan was "Roosevelt, Roche, and Recovery." By contrast, Johnson, her adversary, despised the idea of expanding the federal government in an effort to rescue the country from its economic woes.

Josephine's supporters included the progressive *Rocky Mountain News*. "As a private individual Miss Roche has already accomplished more than most Coloradoans in government," the newspaper said.

But Josephine's lengthy résumé and boundless enthusiasm weren't enough to overcome Johnson's advantage as an incumbent. She narrowly lost the race. Three days later, President Franklin Roosevelt appointed her assistant secretary to the treasury to oversee the US Public Health Service, making her only the second woman ever to hold a subcabinet post. Roosevelt considered Josephine "the very embodiment of the New Deal in Colorado." In her new job she directed fifty-six thousand federal workers in an effort to pull Americans out of poverty.

Josephine resigned in 1937, after her successor as president of Rocky Mountain Fuel died. She returned to Denver hoping to revive the now-ailing company, but it was beyond rescue. Growing numbers of consumers were switching from coal to natural gas, as the latter became more available and less expensive. The company was forced to file for bankruptcy in 1944. When it was resurrected, it ceased mining and focused on owning and managing land, water, and mineral rights. In 2006 it was sold to a private investor.

Bankruptcy trustee Wilbur Newton was quick to point out that Josephine was not to blame for the company's demise. He noted that Rocky Mountain Fuel had accumulated too much debt before she took charge. "She faced an impossible situation for seventeen years," he added. "She did not take the salary from the company she was entitled to, but turned it back. . . . [She] was tireless and unselfish in her efforts to preserve the company as a going business."

Because of her close ties to the United Mine Workers, the union hired Josephine to manage its welfare fund in 1947. The job took her away from Colorado, but she returned periodically for visits. She died in Bethesda, Maryland, on July 29, 1976, at the age of eighty-nine.

Once described by a reporter as a "tiny wisp of a woman whose eyes snap behind tinted glasses," Josephine made an indelible mark not only on the history of Colorado, but also on that of the nation. Most notably, perhaps, she demonstrated that mine managers could cooperate with labor to achieve mutual goals. In their book *Colorado Profiles*, John H. Monnett and Michael McCarthy summed up her contributions this way:

> *Josephine Roche was a woman for all seasons, and her seasons spanned almost the entire social and political life of twentieth-century Colorado. Progressive, New Dealer, laborite—her politics ran like a long, bright thread through the sometimes dark years, and so did her sense of social justice. Josephine Roche was one of Colorado's most brilliant businesswomen and one of its most potent social activists, and she fused the two entities into one of the state's most remarkable personalities. She was, simply, a woman of great grace who believed in the most fundamental of human tenets: That the sanctity of the human spirit was the most important thing in life.*

BIBLIOGRAPHY

General References

Athearn, Robert. *The Coloradans.* Albuquerque: University of New Mexico Press, 1976.

Benson, Maxine. *1001 Colorado Place Names.* Lawrence: University Press of Kansas, 1994.

Monnett, John H., and Michael McCarthy. *Colorado Profiles, Men and Women Who Shaped the Centennial State.* Niwot: University Press of Colorado, 1987.

Peavey, Linda, and Ursula Smith. *Pioneer Women: The Lives of Women on the Frontier.* Rowayton, CT: Saraband, 1996.

Reiter, Joan Swallow. *The Women.* New York: Time-Life Books, 1978.

Robertson, Janet. *The Magnificent Mountain Women: Adventures in the Colorado Rockies.* Lincoln: University of Nebraska Press, 1990.

Schlissel, Lillian. *Women's Diaries of the Westward Journey.* New York: Schocken Books, 1982.

Sherr, Lynn, and Jurate Kazickas. *Susan B. Anthony Slept Here: A Guide to American Women's Landmarks.* New York: Times Books, 1994.

Sprague, Marshall. *Colorado: A Bicentennial History.* New York: W. W. Norton and Co., and American Association for State and Local History, 1976.

Varnell, Jeanne. *Women of Consequence: The Colorado Women's Hall of Fame.* Boulder, CO: Johnson Books, 1999.

Clara Brown

"Aunt Clara Brown Dead." *Denver Tribune Republican,* October 27, 1885, 8.

Bruyn, Kathleen. *Aunt Clara Brown: Story of a Black Pioneer.* Boulder, CO: Pruett Publishing, 1970.

Davidson, Levette J. "Colorado's Hall of Fame." *Colorado Magazine,* vol. 27, January 1950, 23–25.

Editorial. *Denver Republican,* March 17, 1890, 7.

Harvey, James R. "Negroes in Colorado." *Colorado Magazine,* vol. 26, 165–73.

Katz, William Loren. *Black Women of the Old West.* New York: Atheneum Books for Young Readers, 1995.

"Old Aunt Clara Brown, An Aged Colored Woman Who Crossed the Plains in 1859." *Denver Tribune Republican,* June 26, 1885, 2.

Painter, Nell Irvin. *Exodusters: Black Migration to Kansas after the Reconstruction.* New York: Alfred A. Knopf, 1977.

"Pioneers Who Have Gone." *Denver Tribune Republican,* October 28, 1885, 8.

Ravage, John W. *Black Pioneers: Images of the Black Experience on the North American Frontier.* Salt Lake City: University of Utah Press, 1997.

Rice, Arnold S., and John A. Krout. *United States History from 1865.* New York: HarperCollins, 1991.

Elsa Jane Guerin

Chang, Ina. *A Separate Battle: Women and the Civil War.* New York: Scholastic, 1991.

Guerin, E. J. *Mountain Charley, or the Adventures of Mrs. E. J. Guerin, Who Was Thirteen Years in Male Attire.* Introduction by Fred M. Mazzulla and William Kostka. Norman: University of Oklahoma Press, 1968.

Perkin, Robert L. *First Hundred Years: An Informal History of Denver and the* Rocky Mountain News. New York: Doubleday, 1959.

Julia Archibald Holmes

Holmes, Julia Archibald. *A Bloomer Girl on Pikes Peak, 1858.* Edited by Agnes Wright Spring. Denver: A. B. Hirschfeld Press, 1949.

Perkins, Robert L. *First Hundred Years: An Informal History of Denver and the* Rocky Mountain News. New York: Doubleday, 1959.

Scott, James. *Pikes Peak Country.* Helena, MT: Falcon Publishing, 1994.

West, Elliott. *The Contested Plains.* Lawrence: University Press of Kansas, 1998.

Chipeta

Benjamin, Peggy H. "The Last of Captain Jack, a Fresh Appraisal of the Ute Subchief Who Touched Off the Meeker Massacre and Met a Violent Death." *Montana, the Magazine of Western History,* vol. 10, no. 2, Spring 1960, 22–31.

Churchill, Caroline Nichols. *Active Footsteps.* Colorado Springs, CO: Mrs. C. N. Churchill, 1909.

Leckenby, Charles H. *The Tread of Pioneers.* Steamboat Springs, CO: Pilot Press, 1944.

Osborn, Katherine M. B. *Southern Ute Women: Autonomy and Assimilation on the Reservation, 1887–1934.* Albuquerque: University of New Mexico Press, 1998.

Perkin, Robert L. *First Hundred Years: An Informal History of Denver and the* Rocky Mountain News. New York: Doubleday, 1959.

Pettit, Jan. *Utes: The Mountain People.* Boulder, CO: Johnson Books, 1990.

Reagan, Albert B., and Wallace Stark. "Chipeta, Queen of the Utes." *Utah Historical Quarterly,* vol. 6, 1933, 103–11.

Smith, P. David. *Ouray, Chief of the Utes.* Ouray, CO: Wayfinder Press, 1986.

Sprague, Marshall. *Massacre: The Tragedy at White River.* Boston: Little, Brown, 1957.

Trimble, Stephen. *The People: Indians of the American Southwest.* Santa Fe, NM: School of American Research Press, 1993.

Wommack, Linda. *From the Grave: A Roadside Guide to Colorado's Pioneer Cemeteries.* Caldwell, ID: Caxton Press, 1998.

Frances Wisebart Jacobs

Abrams, Jeanne E. *Jewish Denver 1859–1940.* Charleston, SC: Arcadia Publishing, 2007.

———. *Jewish Women Pioneering the Frontier Trail: A History in the American West.* New York: New York University Press, 2006.

Anfenger, Milton L. *The Birth of a Hospital.* Two copies in the Western History Department, Denver Public Library. Publisher not identified, 1942.

Baker, James H., and LeRoy R. Hafen. *History of Colorado.* Denver: Linderman Co., 1927.

Breck, Allen. *The Centennial History of the Jews of Colorado.* Denver: Hirschfeld Press, 1960.

Diner, Hasia R., and Beryl Lieff Benderly. *Her Works Praise Her: A History of Jewish Women in America from Colonial Times to the Present.* New York: Basic Books, 2003.

Hornblein, Marjorie. "Francis Jacobs: Denver's Mother of Charity." *Western States Jewish History, vol. 15, no. 2, January 1983, 131–45.*

James, Edward T., Janet Wilson James, and Paul Boyer. *Notable American Women, 1607–1950: A Biographical Dictionary.* Cambridge, MA, and London: Belknap Press of Harvard University Press, 1971.

Memoir of Mrs. Frances Jacobs of Denver, Colorado: 1843–1892. Denver: Charity Organization Society, 1892.

Ree, Ronald. "Under the Weather: Climate and Disease 1700–1900." *History Today,* vol. 46, no. 1, 1996, 35–41.

Ubbelohde, Carl. *A Colorado History.* Boulder, CO: Pruett Press, 1965.

Uchill, Ida Libert. *Pioneers, Peddlers, and Tsadikim: The Story of the Jews in Colorado.* Boulder, CO: Quality Line Printing, 1979.

Sister Blandina Segale

Becker, Nancy, and Victoria Marie Forde, SC. "Honoring Sister Blandina." *Intercom,* November–December 1998, 5, 10.

Crutchfield, James A., Bill O'Neal, and Dale L. Walker. *Legends of the Wild West.* Lincolnwood, IL: Publications International Ltd., 1997.

Fergusson, Erna. *Our Southwest.* New York: Alfred A. Knopf, 1940.

Forde, Victoria Marie. SC, Sisters of Charity, Mount St. Joseph, Ohio. Letter to author, June 22, 1999.

Hindman, Jane F. *Elizabeth Ann Seton: Mother, Teacher, Saint for Our Time.* New York: Arena Lettres, 1976.

Hurt, Amy Passmore. "Frontier Sister of Courage." *True West,* August 1962, 30–31, 71–72.

Moynihan, Ruth B., Susan Armitage, and Christiane Fischer Dischamp. *So Much to Be Done: Women Settlers on the Mining and Ranching Frontier.* Lincoln: University of Nebraska Press, 1990.

Otto, Robert L. "Nun, 91, Order's Oldest Member, Dies. Formerly Taught in Desert of New Mexico." *Cincinnati Post,* February 24, 1941, 15.

Segal, Alfred. "Cincinnatus." *Cincinnati Post,* February 27, 1941, 10.

Segale, Sister Blandina. *At the End of the Santa Fe Trail.* Sister Therese Martin, ed. Milwaukee: Bruce Publishing, 1948.

Utley, Robert M. "Who Was Billy the Kid?" *Montana: the Magazine of Western History,* vol. 37, no. 3, Summer 1987, 3–11.

Mary Elitch Long

Dier, Caroline Lawrence. *The Lady of the Gardens.* Hollywood, CA: Hollycrofters, 1932.

"Elitch Theatre: History." www.servinghistory.com/topics/Elitch_Theatre::sub:: History.

Faulkner, Debra B. *Mary Elitch Long: First Lady of Fun.* Palmer Lake, CO: Filter Press, 2008.

Gurtler, Jack, Corinne Hunt, and Othniel Sieden. *The Elitch Gardens Story: Memories of Jack Gurtler.* Boulder, CO: Rocky Mountain Writers Guild, 1982.

Hull, Betty Lynne. *Denver's Elitch Gardens: Spinning a Century of Dreams.* Boulder, CO: Johnson Books, 2003.

Long, Mary Elitch. "Memories of Elitch's Gardens Music." *The Echo,* May 1926.

Noel, Tom. "Historic Elitch Theatre Returning to Spotlight." *Rocky Mountain News,* April 26, 2006.

Shepstone, Harold J. "A Woman's Zoo." *Wide World Magazine,* October 1898.

Shikes, Jonathan. "Not-So-New Urbanism: Highlands' Garden Village." *Denver Westword,* June 12, 2009.

Varnell, Jeanne. "Mary Hauck Elitch Long." *Women of Consequence: The Colorado Women's Hall of Fame.* Boulder, CO: Johnson Books, 1999.

Wood, Richard E. *Here Lies Colorado: Fascinating Figures in Colorado History.* Helena, MT: Farcountry Press, 2005.

Florence Sabin

Bluemel, Elinor. *Florence Sabin, Colorado Woman of the Century.* Boulder: University of Colorado Press, 1959.

Flanagan, Mike. *Out West.* New York: Harry N. Abrams, 1987, 91–93.

"Florence Rena Sabin." *Current Biography.* New York: H. W. Wilson, 1945, 527–29.

"Florence Sabin 1871–1953." National Women's Hall of Fame, Seneca Falls, NY, www.greatwomen.org/sabin.htm.

Parkhurst, Genevieve. "Dr. Sabin, Scientist." *Pictorial Review,* January 1930, 2, 70–71.

Phelan, Mary Kay. *Probing the Unknown: The Story of Dr. Florence Sabin.* New York: Thomas Y. Crowell, 1969.

Stoddard, Hope. *Famous American Women.* New York: Thomas Y. Crowell, 1970.

Yost, Edna. *American Women of Science.* Philadelphia and New York: Frederick A. Stokes, 1943.

Martha Maxwell

Barker, Jane Valentine, and Sybil Downing. *Martha Maxwell: Pioneer Naturalist.* Boulder, CO: Pruett Publishing, 1982.

Benson, Maxine. *Martha Maxwell, Rocky Mountain Naturalist.* Lincoln: University of Nebraska Press, 1986.

Dartt, Mary. *On the Plains and Among the Peaks; or How Mrs. Maxwell Made Her Natural History Collection.* Philadelphia: Claxton, Remsen, and Haffelfinger, 1879.

De Lapp, Mary. "Pioneer Woman Naturalist." *Colorado Quarterly,* Summer 1964, 91–96.

Myres, Sandra. *Westering Women and the Frontier Experience.* Albuquerque: University of New Mexico Press, 1982.

Rinhart, Floyd, and Marion Rinhart. "Martha Maxwell's Peaceable Kingdom." *American West,* vol. 13, no. 5, April 1973, 34–35, 62–63.

Caroline Nichols Churchill

Churchill, Caroline Nichols. *Active Footsteps.* Colorado Springs, CO: Mrs. C. N. Churchill, Publisher, 1909.

Myres, Sandra L. *Westering Women and the Frontier Experience 1800–1915.* Albuquerque: University of New Mexico Press, 1982.

Rumsey, Becky. "Western Women Wild with Joy!" *High Country News,* December 13, 1993, 8–9.

Elizabeth "Baby" Doe Tabor

Arvidson, Millie, manager of Matchless Mine–Baby Doe Tabor Museum, Leadville, Colorado. Phone interview, November 22, 1999.

Bancroft, Caroline. *Silver Queen: The Fabulous Story of Baby Doe Tabor.* Boulder, CO: Johnson Publishing, 1953.

———. *Augusta Tabor: Her Side of the Scandal.* Boulder, CO: Johnson Publishing, 1955.

Burke, John. *The Legend of Baby Doe: The Colorful Life and Times of the Silver Queen of the West.* New York: G. P. Putnam's Sons, 1974.

Chase, Robert. "Baby Doe Dies at Her Post Guarding Matchless Mine." *Rocky Mountain News,* March 8, 1935, 1.

Flanagan, Mike. *Out West.* New York: Harry N. Abrams, 1987.

Hafen, LeRoy R., ed. *Colorado and Its People: A Narrative and Topical History of the Centennial State.* New York: Lewis Historical Publishing, 1948.

Hall, Gordon Langley. *The Two Lives of Baby Doe.* Philadelphia: Macrae Smith, 1962.

Perkin, Robert L. *The First Hundred Years: An Informal History of Denver and the Rocky Mountain News.* New York: Doubleday & Co., 1959.

Smith, Duane A. *Horace Tabor: His Life and the Legend.* Boulder: Colorado Associated University Press, 1973.

Stone, Irving. *Men to Match My Mountains: The Opening of the Far West, 1840–1900.* Garden City, NY: Doubleday & Co., 1956.

Temple, Judy Nolte. *Baby Doe Tabor: The Madwoman in the Cabin.* Norman: University of Oklahoma Press, 2007.

Polly Pry

"Condition of Mr. Bonfils and Mr. Tammen." *Denver Post,* January 15, 1900, 1–2.

Davis, Kenneth C. *Don't Know Much About History: Everything You Need to Know about American History but Never Learned.* New York: Crown Publishers, 1990.

Fowler, Gene. *Timber Line.* Garden City, NY: Garden City Publishing, 1933.

Hodges, Eva. "The Adventures of Polly Pry." *Denver Post,* February 18, 1968, 6–7.

Iversen, Kristen. *Molly Brown: Unraveling the Myth.* Boulder, CO: Johnson Books, 1999.

Pence, Mary Lou. "Polly Pry." In *The Women Who Made the West.* Garden City, NY: Doubleday, 1980, 104–119.

Ross, Ishbel. *Ladies of the Press: The Story of Women in Journalism by an Insider.* New York: Harper & Brothers, 1936.

"The Shooting of Messrs. Bonfils and Tammen." *Denver Post;* January 14, 1900; 1–2.

"So the People May Know." *Denver Post,* January 16, 1900, 1.

Ubbelohde, Carl, Maxine Benson, and Duane Smith. *A Colorado History.* Boulder, CO: Pruett Publishing, 1972.

Ann Bassett and Josie Bassett

Boren, Kerry Ross. "A personal interview with Josie Bassett." www.prospector-utah.com/bassett.htm.

"Josie Bassett Morris." Pamphlet published by Dinosaur National Monument, Dinosaur, CO, 1989.

Leckenby, Charles H. *The Tread of Pioneers.* Steamboat Springs, CO: Pilot Press, 1944.

Mancini, Richard. *American Legends of the Wild West.* Philadelpia: Courage Books, 1992.

McClure, Grace. *The Bassett Women.* Athens: Ohio University Press/Swallow Press, 1985.

Patterson, Richard. *Butch Cassidy, a Biography.* Lincoln: University of Nebraska Press, 1998.

Ubbelohde, Carl, Maxine Benson, and Duane Smith. *A Colorado History.* Boulder, CO: Pruett Publishing, 1972.

Willis, Ann Bassett. "Queen Ann of Brown's Park." *Colorado Magazine,* April 1952, 81–98; July 1952, 218–235; October 1952, 284–298; and January 1953, 58–76.

Wommack, Linda. *From the Grave: A Roadside Guide to Colorado's Pioneer Cemeteries.* Caldwell, ID: Caxton Press, 1998.

Zwinger, Ann. *Run, River, Run.* New York: Harper & Row, 1975.

Margaret Tobin Brown

Bancroft, Caroline. *The Unsinkable Mrs. Brown.* Denver: Golden Press, 1956.

Dorset, Phyllis Flanders. *The New Eldorado: The Story of Colorado's Gold and Silver Rushes.* New York: Macmillan, 1970.

Flanagan, Mike. *Out West.* New York: Harry N. Abrams, 1987.

Fowler, Gene. *Timber Line.* Garden City, NY: Garden City Publishing, 1933.

Harbold, Laura. "Beyond Unsinkable: The Real Molly Brown" Humanities, vol. 28, no. 3, May/June 2007.

Iversen, Kristen. *Molly Brown: Unraveling the Myth.* Boulder, CO: Johnson Books, 1999.

Lord, Walter. *A Night to Remember.* New York: Bantam, 1977.

"Molly Brown, An American Original." *Biography,* A&E Network. Originally broadcast November 6, 1998.

Semple, James Alexander. *Representative Women of Colorado.* Denver: Alexander Art Publishing, 1914.

Ubbelohde, Carl, Maxine Benson, and Duane Smith. *A Colorado History.* Boulder, CO: Pruett Publishing, 1972.

Whitacre, Christine. *Molly Brown: Denver's Unsinkable Lady.* Denver: Historic Denver, 1984.

Josephine Roche

Armstrong, Gerald R. "Miss Josephine Roche, President, The Rocky Mountain Fuel Company, 1927–1951." Report to Rocky Mountain Fuel Company shareholders, April 14, 1975.

Barrett, Marjorie. "Josephine Roche: She Fuels an Historic Era of Area History." *Rocky Mountain News,* April 20, 1975, 15.

Chernow, Ron. *Titan: The Life of John D. Rockefeller, Sr.* New York: Random House, 1998.

Fong, Tillie. "Capitalist and Humanitarian." From Colorado Millennium 2000 website. Sponsored by *Rocky Mountain News,* NEWS 4, and Colorado Historical Society. (Website no longer active.)

———. "Capitalist and Humanitarian." Rocky Mountain News, July 13, 1999. http://denver.rockymountainnews.com/millennium/0713mile.shtml.

Halaas, David Fridtjof. "Josephine Roche, 1886–1976: Social Reformer, Mine Operator." *Colorado Heritage News,* March 1985, 4.

"On Losing Side." *Business Week,* April 28, 1945, 72.

Rice, Arnold S., and John A. Krout. *United States History from 1865.* New York: HarperCollins, 1991.

"Roosevelt, Roche, and Recovery." *Literary Digest,* September 1, 1934, 8.

Vandenbusche, Duane, and Duane A. Smith. *A Land Alone: Colorado's Western Slope.* Boulder, CO: Pruett Publishing, 1981.

INDEX

ABOUT THE AUTHOR

Gayle C. Shirley launched TwoDot's More Than Petticoats series in 1995 with her popular book on remarkable Montana women born before 1900. She's the author of several other books, including *Four-Legged Legends of Colorado, Charlie's Trail: The Life and Art of C. M. Russell,* and *More Than Petticoats: Remarkable Oregon Women.* She lives with her husband and two sons in Helena, Montana, where she finds it especially easy to indulge her passion for western history.